Tarot
Court Cards

For Beginners

Bring Clarity to Your Readings

LEEZA ROBERTSON

Llewellyn Publications
Woodbury, Minnesota

About the Author

Leeza Robertson spends more time with tarot cards than with real-life people. You will find her hidden away in warm, cozy corners with piles of decks and books around her. She spends her days dreaming up new decks and exploring ways to introduce more people to the world of tarot. When she doesn't have her nose inside a book or her fingers dancing across a deck of cards, she runs her online class called the Moonbeamers, which focuses on tarot and the moon's cycles. Connect with her on Twitter (@Leeza_Robertson) or email: leezarobertsontarot@gmail.com.

To Write to the Author

If you wish to contact the author or would like more information about this book, please write to the author in care of Llewellyn Worldwide, and we will forward your request. Both the author and publisher appreciate hearing from you and learning of your enjoyment of this book and how it has helped you. Llewellyn Worldwide cannot guarantee that every letter written to the author can be answered, but all will be forwarded. Please write to:

Leeza Robertson
℅ Llewellyn Worldwide
2143 Wooddale Drive
Woodbury, MN 55125-2989

Please enclose a self-addressed stamped envelope for reply,
or $1.00 to cover costs. If outside the USA, enclose
an international postal reply coupon.

contents

First Edition
First Printing, 2017

Book format: Bob Gaul
Cover art: Llewellyn's Classic Tarot by Barbara Moore and Eugene Smith
  © 2014, Llewellyn Publications
Cover design: Lisa Novak
Editing: Laura Graves
Tarot decks used in this publication:
Gaian Tarot by Joanna Powell Colbert © 2011, Llewellyn Publications
Tarot of the Hidden Realm by Barbara Moore and Julia Jeffrey © 2013,
  Llewellyn Publications
Llewellyn Classic Tarot by Barbara Moore and Eugene Smith © 2014,
  Llewellyn Publications
Interior card spreads: Llewellyn art department

Llewellyn Publications is a registered trademark of Llewellyn Worldwide Ltd.

Library of Congress Cataloging-in-Publication Data (Pending)
ISBN: 978-0-7387-5016-3

Llewellyn Worldwide Ltd. does not participate in, endorse, or have any authority or responsibility concerning private business transactions between our authors and the public.

All mail addressed to the author is forwarded, but the publisher cannot, unless specifically instructed by the author, give out an address or phone number.

Any Internet references contained in this work are current at publication time, but the publisher cannot guarantee that a specific location will continue to be maintained. Please refer to the publisher's website for links to authors' websites and other sources.

Llewellyn Publications
A Division of Llewellyn Worldwide Ltd.
2143 Wooddale Drive
Woodbury, MN 55125-2989
www.llewellyn.com

Printed in the United States of America

introduction

Ask newcomers to tarot which cards they struggle with the most when it comes to learning the deck, and nine out of ten will say the court cards. For whatever reason, these people or face cards tend to prove quite the challenge to many an aspiring tarot reader. I have to admit that even I struggled with these cards in the beginning, and it wasn't until I came across Mary K. Greer and Tom Little's *The Tarot Court* that things started to make a modicum of sense. Even then, it wasn't enough for me to truly build a deep relationship with the cards themselves; I needed to break it down so even a two-year-old could understand it. Slowly but surely, I was able to build a multilayered scholastic approach to what are now my new favorite cards in any tarot deck.

The path I traveled to the court cards is in every page of this book. Not only will I walk you through my own process,

I will also share exercises and lessons I have taught to tarot newbies and veterans alike for years. Before that, let's get something clear: this is a book designed with a beginner in mind, and even though I do offer some "beyond beginner" tips and exercises, this is really for those of you struggling to make sense of these sixteen cards. That said, this book is meant to work with Rider-Waite-Smith-inspired tarot decks as I will be looking at them as the primary source of understanding. There are also sections in this book dedicated to members of the royal court from Thoth-influenced decks. So no matter what sort of deck you hold in your hands, your members of court will be mentioned.

Many new readers are coming to the world of tarot with new and modern decks, and I do understand that the imagery and sometimes the names have changed, however the principles of the court remain very much the same. It was therefore very important for me to find a nice selection of imagery to work with in this book. The decks I have selected to use as examples throughout the following chapters illustrate the traditional imagery from the Rider-Waite-Smith, mystical interpretations, as well as gender-bending beliefs related to archetypal energy. The decks we will explore in this book are Llewellyn's Classic Tarot, the Gaian Tarot, and the Tarot of the Hidden Realm. These decks not only give you a fantastic array of images to explore the court cards with, but they will also show you how the same card can be expressed in three very different ways. That variety is part of learning about all the people, as they have different components to who they are and show up differently depending on situations and expectations.

I know only too well how frustrating learning the court cards can be. But I also know how amazing it is to have them as allies and friends. I want you to become best friends with the members of the tarot court because, like all good friends, they will challenge you, encourage you, and give you the best advice you could ever hope to hear. So without further ado, let's continue with the introductions.

In chapter 1 you will be introduced to the many faces of the court's pages. You will find notes on the princesses and reference to this card as an elemental child. Next we will move on to the knights and princes. There is more to learn in this chapter than the others as the knights themselves are complex and multifaceted. Chapter 3 will bring you to the four queens of the tarot kingdom. You will see by the end of this chapter just how important these cards are even today. Chapter 5 brings us to the top seat in the tarot kingdom, the kings. These kings are more than just leaders, and you will learn more about the many roles they must fill in order to keep their crowns.

Each chapter ends with two connection exercises. One is a journal or meditation exercise and the other is a spread specific to the cards in general. These spreads and exercises are to assist you becoming closer to the people these cards represent as well as their gifts and guidance. Chapter 6 brings it all together by bringing in the rest of the players in the complete tarot empire. This chapter also includes instructions on how to create your own court cards so you can deepen your connection to them even further.

You will find all you will need to begin your journey with these sixteen cards right here, in this book. When you feel ready to deepen your knowledge and go further with your reading skills and knowledge, consider reading the books listed in the Recommended Reading section. There you will find not just tarot books but also books that will allow you to tap into the specific qualities of each court card.

So grab those court cards and begin your journey into the four kingdoms of the tarot empire.

one

A Brief History of the Tarot

Generations honor generations endlessly.
Cultivated in the self, virtue is realized;
cultivated in the family, virtue overflows;
cultivated in the community, virtue increases;
cultivated in the state, virtue abounds.

THE DAO DE JING, VERSE 54

. . . .

It is not uncommon for most tarot books to start with a brief history of tarot, but here we are going to explore only the court cards. If you want to walk into the depths of tarot's mysterious beginnings, there are plenty of fabulous books to choose from (see Recommended Reading). In order for you to truly connect with the sixteen cards of the tarot court, you have to forget that the other cards exist. Think of it as though you yourself are entering court life. You have traveled across land and sea; the life you once knew is now far behind you. The only way for you to survive is to learn the lessons of the new world you now find yourself in. Like it or not, these sixteen cards are all you have for now.

But where did they come from, and how did we end up with these four very distinct families?

The royals first made their appearance on playing cards sometime in the mid-fifteenth century in Europe, which was around about the time the War of the Roses broke out. This historic war was a dynastic battle for the throne of England that would change the monarchy forever. These earliest cards showed the kings, queens, knights, and knaves, and they were much the same as we see them today on decks of regular playing cards. They were also broken into four distinct suits.

Not long after these first decks appeared, they evolved into a card game called *trionfi* and the additional trump or major arcana cards were added. Like most forms of divination, the tarot really became prominent in the eighteenth century. This was also around the time that royal courts started to change, and the role of the knight was in decline. By the time the Rider-Waite-Smith deck was published in 1910, the power of the royal court was all but gone and the world was a very different place indeed. It is no wonder that these days we find it harder to connect with these cards than the people of the fifteenth century did.

Basic Tarot Terminology

Like most mysterious things, tarot has its own language. There are even words used in tarot specific to the user. Following is a small list of words you will see in other books about tarot as well as hear them from many readers. If you are very new to the world of tarot, I suggest paying particular attention, but don't panic if it takes you a while or worry if you yourself never end up using these words. To be honest, it took me years to figure out who or what a querent was, I kid you not. I always wondered if it had something to do with Harry Potter, because to be fair, it sounded like a word that would be used in the Harry Potter universe. It wasn't until I attended an online class with Rachel Pollack (the matriarch of tarot) that it finally all came together. For the record, I have never uses the word "querent" to this day…unless I am writing books like this one.

- *Reader*—the person conducting the tarot session. This person not only acts as a medium between your question and your answer, this person literally reads the cards that end up in front of them.

- *Reading*—the process of answering a given question, showing a strategic approach in and around a current situation, or guiding the inquirer through the many possibilities that now present themselves in their current "right now" life.

- *Querent*—the person who comes to the reader. This person asks the questions or is otherwise seeking a solution or answer to a specific question or concern.

- *Archetype*—a symbolic or personality type. For example, the king is an archetype of power, leadership, and control.

- *Spread*—a particular way of laying out the cards to get to a specific point of inquiry or to find the appropriate solution to a problem.

- *Divination*—a way to foresee future events or to understand underlying knowledge and omens through a magical process.

- *Arcana*—specialized knowledge and the pursuit of higher wisdom.

Suit and Rank

If you are new to tarot or just starting out on your tarot journey, you will soon see that the minor arcana is divided into four suits: cups, pentacles or disks, wands, and swords. Each suit corresponds to an element: cups align to the element of water, pentacles or disks align to the element of earth, wands aligns to the element of fire, and swords aligns to the element of air. When it comes to new and more modern tarot decks, the suits may not always be called or depict cups, wands, pentacles, and swords, but they do generally align to their corollary element. So if you do have a deck that has different names for suits, you can always find out what it is by what element each represents. One of the tricks I taught myself when I first started my tarot journey was to see each of the suits as their own kingdom or realm. This method also helped me learn my way around the court cards much faster.

Think of it like the kingdom of cups as the guardians of water, emotional well-being, and creation energy. It is their responsibility to care for, tend to, and maintain these watery elements throughout the empire of tarot. The kingdom of pentacles is the guardians of our physical resources; things like money, food, health care, and tending to the earth are their responsibilities. The kingdom of wands is guardians of fire, passion, and action; they are all about getting things done. The kingdom of swords is the guardians of air; they maintain logic and reason and hold the space for higher learning in the empire.

Here is a short list of keywords that will assist you even further with each of the suits:

- *Cups*—emotions, intuition, flow, love, creation, reflection, mirror, dreams, friendship, romance, birth, moon, healing, subconscious mind, letting go, visions

- *Pentacles*—the physical body, money, personal items, security, stability, foundation, safety, hoarding, value, outer world, touch, taste, feel, smell, physical work

- *Wands*—energy, inspiration, passion, creativity, action, goals, risk, movement, desire, manifestation, speed, arrogance, revenge, anger, heat, warmth

- *Swords*—logic, study, philosophy, decisions, thinking, stress, anxiety, analyzing, higher learning, reason, will, cutting through the crap, swift justice

Each suit or kingdom has a part to play in a very strategic way. This also makes the roles of those pesky sixteen cards easier to deal with as well, as each plays a very key role in the kingdom they live in and govern. Let's face it, we all have very specific skills and these skills are in demand, but you need to know when, where, and how to use your divine gift. This is the true role the court cards play. They not only define the roles but also show you how to play them and when.

So let's take a look at the rank and file:

- *Kings*—these are the leaders of the kingdom. The head honchos and commanders-in-chief of the element they govern. This means they are also masters at using their chosen element (more on that in later chapters).

- *Queens*—where the kings lead, the queens network. These ladies are all about building relationships and making sure that the gifts of the realm keep on giving.

- *Knights/Princes*—in Rider-Waite-Smith-influenced decks, you will find knights. These are the defenders of the realm and protectors of their kingdoms. In Thoth-influenced decks, you will find princes instead of knights; they represent a more adolescent energy whose role will be discussed in later chapters.

- *Pages/Princesses*—the page, the lowest in the court rankings of Rider-Waite-Smith-influenced decks, is the youngest and has the most to learn. In the Thoth-inspired decks, you will see this role taken up by the princess. We shall discuss the princess and the page more in later chapters.

But to truly start to understand this rank and file system, you have to start the journey at the top. Because to be honest this is where the confusion of the beginner really sets in. In order to understand the sixteen court cards you must first understand the role of the highest ruling powers in the land, the Emperor and his Empress.

The Role of the Emperor and Empress

High in the major arcana, seated in the front for all to see are the Empress and the Emperor. They are the highest rank that one can have in a monarchy. But here is where it can get confusing: an emperor can also be a king, but he doesn't have to be a king in order to be an emperor. Likewise, an empress can also be a queen but doesn't need to be a queen in order to take up her title as empress. Don't be fooled into thinking that this confusion is a simple matter of semantics—there is a very real difference between the power of the emperor and the role of the king.

The best way to go from here is to understand that the tarot itself is a vast and wondrous land. It is so vast that the emperor who controls all of it cannot rule it on his own. He just cannot be in all places at once, so he keeps the regional aristocracy in power to maintain the kingdoms. The kingdom of wands in the east, the kingdom of cups in the west, the kingdom of pentacles in the north, and the kingdom of swords in the south. But it is the emperor alone who gets the final say on things within the land of tarot, for his power is absolute. This system is how I both learned the court cards and how I like to teach them. Please understand that you do not have to adopt this way of thinking about the court cards in order to work with them or get to know them better. I have just found that this system makes it easier for most.

Today in the land outside of tarot, the world that you and I live in, there is only one remaining real-life emperor, the emperor of Japan. Although he is more a figurehead than an emperor of old, he and his empress are the last connection we have to a way of life that many of our ancestors endured. Today's version of the emperor and empress take up their power in suits and ties; we call them CEOs. The corporate world is the only real place where mergers, hostile takeovers, and territorial disputes play out. The constant grabbing for more power and more money is the realm of the post-modern emperors and empresses. Instead of the battlefield, the board-room has become the new battleground. It seems fitting, really, as this energy has to have somewhere to go.

Another way to think of this tarot empire is to view the emperor and empress as the whole package, a complete and total ruling couple, and the kings and queens of the suits as parts of their personality: the cups, emotional; the wands, active; the swords, intellectual processing; and pentacles, physical resources. In this scenario, the royal families of the minor arcana become inner archetypes of the emperor and empress. You might have to move beyond the basics just a wee bit to wrap your head around this one, but it makes more sense when you get the Emperor card and one of the kings in the same reading, as it can suggest how to deal with your role as leader or what area of your current situation needs to be managed or governed.

Look at the following example from Llewellyn's Classic Tarot. We see a simple three-card spread, and in it are the Emperor, the King of Cups, and the 8 of Swords. In this spread we could say that in order for you to learn the lesson of the 8 of Swords, you need to control or govern your emotions. Or another way to read the spread would be: leading with your emotions in check brings about a more intuitive release. Or in order to lead by example, you are going to have to tap into your creative skills and find a new way of experiencing the world around you. No matter how you read these three cards—and trust me, I could go on and on about how to interpret what they say—the king acts as the personality type or inner archetype to the emperor in this spread. This rule can also be applied to the empress. If she shows up next to one of the queens, you can follow the same formula.

The Emperor **King of Cups** **8 of Swords**

Three-Card Spread (Llewellyn's Classic Tarot)

The Empress in the tarot seems to have evolved into a very different woman than the real-life empresses throughout history. Only one element of them seems to remain the same, the vessel through which life is created and born. Pick up any history book and you will see just how bad these woman had it.

They were sent off to unknown lands to secure territories that they could not have cared less about, to have children they would never raise in order to secure some stranger's bloodline—all in all a pretty damn horrifying experience. The story of Catherine II is a great example of this. Once she finally rid herself of her horrid husband, Peter III (called "the Great"), she spent the rest of her life screwing her way through all the handsome men of the Russian court. She never governed, not once. Instead she handed positions of power off to her ex-lovers as payment for their work in the bedroom. This real example hardly matches up with the Divine Mother archetype we find in the major arcana.

The Empress of the tarot empire has been reinvented over and over again, more so than her spouse, the Emperor. One has to wonder if this is because more women are now creating tarot decks and are more instrumental in how they want to see these archetypes tell the story of feminine energy. Because let's face it, who wants to be associated with the awful life of real, historic empresses? As we begin to move into an age where the labels of gender are being questioned as valid, it will be interesting to see how the Empress and her husband will evolve in future decks. Even today it is not advisable to see each of the gendered cards as set in stone. In my own tarot classes, I ask students to explore the personality traits of each of the court cards rather than the gender. You will notice this theme of gender fluidity throughout the rest of this book, and this mindset should also help when it comes to taking on the role of a card that you do not consider your natural state of identification.

Who Is This Card?

One of the biggest causes for confusion when dealing with the court cards is knowing who the cards are in the reading. Who exactly do they represent? When I was first learning the tarot, I was told that a court card represented someone who shared the likeness of the card itself. In other words, if I got a king, it was referring to an actual man in my life who looked and carried himself like the king in the cards. This was beyond confusing to me as I just didn't have any men in my life and still don't! My friends are all women, my clients are all women, and I am married to a woman.

So who the hell were all of these men? It turns out that the kings I kept seeing in my readings were actually me—they were showing a role that I personally was meant to step into. This is now how I teach the court cards. Consider them as being you until more evidence proves otherwise because sometimes they really do represent other people in our lives. That said, believe it or not, most times they do not.

My aim here is for you to have more than enough information about each of the court cards, such that you will know beyond a shadow of a doubt if a court card is you or someone else in your life. Even if the gender on the card doesn't match the gender of the person, you will still be able to identify them in a reading. For example, as you will see in the section on queens, a lot of men can show up in a reading as queens, strange but true. There will be other times when the position or roles and responsibilities of a specific court card are important for you to adapt to and learn to find the answer or result you seek.

Here's my hot tip (okay, it's not *that* hot): When in doubt, the card is you. Always presume it is you first until proven otherwise.

two

The Pages, Princesses, and Children

Tell me and I forget
Teach me and I will remember
Involve me and I will learn

BENJAMIN FRANKLIN

. . . .

In the world of tarot, the page can go by other names: the child, the maiden, the daughter, or the novice, to name but a few. It is the youngest, more naive member of the family. In decks created from the Thoth school of tarot, you will see this card come up as the princess. Yet no matter which name this card seems to have, its energy is very similar. It is the card that indicates youth, a lack of real-world understanding, and a lot of room for growth and expansion. In this chapter the focus will be on the two main tarot schools and their depictions of this elemental child, the page and the princess.

History, Myth, and Legend

Page—Historically speaking, a page in the royal court would have been male, as a page was a squire in training. Pages tended to range in age from seven to twelve years old. They were taken in by royal or noble families to work and train to become knights. Being a knight was the ultimate goal for any young boy in the time of feudal rule. We see this representation of the page in Llewellyn's Classic Tarot. All the pages in this particular deck are young men actively learning the ways of the suit or kingdom in which they would have been employed.

As tarot has evolved, so too has the representation of the page. In modern day tarot, pages are not only male—they can also be female. Gender itself is not as important as the many different ways the story of the page can be told. And it can be told in many fabulous and creative ways. Both the Tarot of the Hidden Realm and the Gaian Tarot show us page cards that are not limited by gender, giving a unique twist on the tale of the tarot page.

The job of the historical page was a tedious and boring one. They were given the lowliest of tasks around the castle or noble house. Their duties were mundane and oftentimes mind-numbing. But these tasks allowed the page to learn very specific skills in a very refined and regimented way. They did the same thing over and over and over again. Active repetition entrenched habits and instilled behaviors into them in a way that no amount of telling or reading alone could ever possibly accomplish. This is something all the pages share in common, making them wonderful study buddies.

The four pages of the tarot court are learning the lessons of their individual elements, starting from scratch. They are practicing day in and day out some of the most basic yet essential skills they will need to progress to the next level of their growth or training. The pages remind me of a Zen koan: "Before enlightenment: chop wood, carry water. After enlightenment: chop wood, carry water." No matter where we are in our lives, we never stop needing the most basic of skills, and at some point we will find ourselves back at the beginning, starting once again from scratch.

The pages may be only children, but they have so much to teach and share with us. All we have to do is listen.

Princess—Unlike the page, the princess was not sent to live at the castle or house of nobility; she was born and raised there. She was educated and groomed from birth for a very specific purpose. She already has a place in royal society and doesn't have to prove anything to anyone. That does not make her lessons any less important than the page's, however. If anything, she carries much more weight on her shoulders, especially if she is the only daughter to be married off to secure land, allies, and better trade routes. Some princesses were engaged before they could even walk. Alliances in the Middle Ages were crucial, and matches would have been made long before a young princess had a chance to think about making any life decisions on her own.

The princesses of history had no say in their own lives. They were vessels, bought and traded and very little more.

Their lives were very rarely happy and they were bound by duty and honor. In fact, we don't have to look too far back in time to see how being a princess can ruin your life. The life and death of Princess Diana Spencer was a modern tragedy that shocked the world and touched people who were not even part of the commonwealth governed by the British monarchy. Even sadder, what Diana experienced was far better than all the princesses who came before her.

In my humble opinion, I think Disney has done a real number on the retelling of the princess story. Pick any Disney princess, and you would think that being the daughter of the king or queen was the most magical thing that could ever happen to you. The truth is so far removed from the world of Disney, it might just make you want to run away and rock in the corner for a while. The reality is that princesses were usually doomed. Very few of them actually became queens and even fewer lived long lives. And God forbid if you came from a family that only seemed to produce girls. Being the last princess in a family of princesses pretty much meant you were handed off to whomever would have you.

George R. R. Martin's very popular *A Song of Ice and Fire* series and television show *Game of Thrones* has done a much better job of showing court life than Disney ever has. Throughout history, a happy ending for a princess was not at all expected; it wasn't even expected she would survive past her wedding night. Imagine frightened young girls married off to older, crazier, and often violent men. They were often treated as their husbands saw fit, oftentimes meaning rape, beatings, imprisonment in their rooms, starvation, and being "offered" to other members of court. Does being a real-life princess sound fun to you? I would have preferred being a page!

To be fair, not all princesses experienced a dismal life. Some actually moved on to become powerful queens who challenged the status quo and became a part of the ever-growing women's revolution. Elizabeth I of England, the first by rights, should never have seen the throne: she was a princess from a second marriage, quite removed from regal succession. Really, she was lucky to have kept her head. But she would go on to become one of the most powerful woman kings (a role different from a queen) in history. As for our princess and her unknown future, she still needs to learn how to rule, how to maintain power, and most of all how to lead. All are important and necessary skills for navigating life in general.

Page of Pentacles: Child of Earth

Forget not that the earth delights to feel your bare feet and the winds long to play with your hair.

KHALIL GIBRAN

Personification of Earth
Zodiac Signs: Taurus, Virgo, Capricorn
Keywords: Careful, practical, consistent

As a person

Page—The Page of Pentacles is the youngest member of the pentacles court, usually aged somewhere between eight and twelve. He is curious but cautious by nature and prefers to be outside. In fact, this child does much better outdoors than indoors. Watching the natural world and observing its patterns is one of this page's favorite pastimes. This young page will often have an affinity with animals and when indoors, nature shows and animal programs will often be the preferred choice. It is not uncommon for this page to be very knowledgeable about the natural world and have a head full of facts and figures about animals, trees, and geographical locations you many never have heard of.

These pages tend to be good with their hands, especially when it comes to building things and pulling them apart. Food is also an important element of their experience. We often forget that food comes from the earth. Growing, harvesting, and preparing our food is grounding and earth-binding. This child of earth will learn early what plants he or she can and cannot eat and won't wait for permission to go and help him- or herself to the bounty. (One thing this page won't do is go hungry!) Which makes the Page of Pentacles a nice friend to have if you ever find yourself in need of a snack. Case in point, take a closer look at the page card from the Gaian Tarot, the Child of Earth. The apple depicted may have a special symbolic meaning, but rest assured that child is going to eat it—with or without your permission.

Princess—When I think about the Princess of Pentacles, I think of a strong, stubborn young lady who won't be rushed. She is one of those children who knows exactly what she will be when she grows up and won't be deterred by how long it may take. She spends a lot of time outside and prefers the company of animals over people. Her ally and confidante is more than likely her pet, which she brings with her everywhere she goes. There is no doubt that this little princess has been called a tomboy more than once in her life; she wears it like a badge of honor.

Some people may call this princess a bit of a wild child, but the truth is that she just dances to a different beat: the beat of the earth, which is slow, long, and enduring. Much like the image we see in the Tarot of the Hidden Realm, this child is close to the earth. It's almost as if they are one. Perhaps you have come across Princess of Pentacles people. They are less concerned with time than most because they understand the nature of cycles. They tend to keep track of the sun more than their watch. They always seem to be outside somewhere and are usually alone. Although this princess is very social, she really does value quiet alone time.

As an archetypal influence

Page—The child of the earth has much to learn, but also much to teach. The child of the earth is still very much full of wonder and has yet to be hardened by the world around it. The child of the earth is still connected to that which created it, which means it still believes in magic. This is important when dealing with this card as an archetypal influence.

Let me give you a real-life example: Before I go to a business conference, I always do a reading. I ask what sort of things I should focus on while at the conference, what benefits I should be on the lookout for, and who I should be as I attend the conference. Nine times out of ten I will get the Page of Pentacles as who I need to be while attending the conference. I kid you not, I am always asked by the universe/god/goddess/creator, whatever you call it, to go in and be a child of the earth. When the page shows up like this, it lets me know I will learn a lot from what will be offered. It is also a humbling reminder that I am going in as a student, not master, and should leave that chip on my shoulder at the door.

When working with archetypes, it is important to remember that they also have a shadow side. When we apply it to the cards, we say we are working with card reversals. The reverse aspect or shadow side of the Page of Pentacles would be a very stubborn and selfish energy. Just think of a toddler throwing a temper tantrum. My brother would be the role model for the reversal of this card. When he was a toddler, he used to throw the most amazing public temper tantrums I have ever seen. It would be complete with throwing himself on the floor, right under a security camera, and wailing so loudly that you could hear him four stores down. He was the master of the tantrum; he really should have won some sort of trophy. But this is the shadow aspect of the card: a petulant, entitled know-it-all who has no respect or regard for the material world in which he or she lives. I am pretty sure we can agree on the fact that you don't have to be a toddler to revel in that sort of energy!

Princess—I have to admit that I love the idea of seeing a young Princess of Pentacles as the bright-eyed girl with a dream to open her own business, start a new company, or someone who now finds the need to reinvent themselves after life has thrown them a curve ball. Unlike the page, she already has a few connections she can draw on if and when she needs them. So even though she may be starting at the bottom, she is not doing it without support. Think of her sort of like a young Kate Hudson, but you really don't need to have that sort of money behind you to use this princess as an archetype.

The popular perception is that women think differently about resources than men, although that notion is changing. Over the past few years, we have seen more and more financial coaches who are women become prominent figures. Think Suze Orman and Barbara Stanny. So if this card has shown itself in a reading, you might want to take a closer look at where your money comes from and where it goes. Just as the page is taught to be mindful of the chain of supply and demand, the Princess of Pentacles also needs to pay attention to these lessons.

The Princess of Pentacles is a wonderful card to work with if you are at the start of anything pertaining to the suit of pentacles. Be it a new business, a new health and wellness regime, that long overdue savings account, a retirement account, an investment portfolio, cooking lessons, or time management training, the princess encourages you to use the resources you have at your disposal, be it people, places, or things to accelerate your progress.

You might also want to keep track of your time, exercise, and diet as well. Abundance is a divine right, but if you don't know what to do with the abundance you already have, how will you know what to do with what is to come?

As a spiritual influence

In Llewellyn's Classic Tarot, the Page of Pentacles is a very interesting page indeed. Look closely and you will notice that he is not even touching his pentacle. Instead it floats in front of him. In a field full of life and abundance, the young page is learning all about his connection to the divine supply. It is around the ages of eight and twelve that you would have cemented your thoughts, feelings, and beliefs around your own personal divine supply. To be fair, however, none of those feelings, beliefs, or thoughts would have actually been yours.

Money is an essential part of the physical experience. Whether we like it or not, it is necessary for our daily experience. Yet money itself is nothing more than energy, a divine flow. Money may have been called the root of all evil, but it is really a sacred and spiritual tool. All lessons around it are part and parcel of spiritual growth and expansion. When the Page of Pentacles comes up in a reading, the cards may be alerting you to a money block or inner childhood belief related to money and abundance. Note that money and abundance are not the same thing, although money does fall under the abundance umbrella.

What thoughts, feelings and beliefs do you have around money? Do you feel like it is constantly out of reach, like the pentacle appears to be for the Page of Pentacles?

Have you ever caught yourself verbalizing that there is never enough to go around? How about your bills? Do you enjoy receiving them and believe paying them is a form of gratitude? Or do you hate looking at them and feel anger and annoyance when you pay them, as if someone is taking something from you? Are you so blessed with divine supply that you wrap your money in love and gratitude?

Keep in mind these money patterns have been with you long before you were ever in control of your own divine supply. This is important, as the Page of Pentacles offers up a healing and clearing point around the beliefs that were given to you and the ones that are actually yours. This healing and clearing is necessary so there is no inner conflict between your true thoughts, feelings, and beliefs and those handed down to you.

Not everyone will have money blocks, but that does not mean they don't have abundance blocks. Abundance comes in many wonderful forms: time, health, love, happiness, pleasure, opportunity, and freedom, just to name a few. Do you have issues with one or more of these? I know a lot of people who have an abundance of money yet struggle with pleasure, time, and health. Blocks in any one of these abundance areas will put a kink in your divine supply hose.

Once you have identified which area of abundance is causing you to feel stuck or blocked, use the Page of Pentacles as a point of healing. Sit with the card and use it as a focus for meditation. Tell this child of the earth all of your hopes and dreams. Say what you would do if you had no abundance excuses. See yourself become one with this page and join together in a shared sacred lesson of aligning oneself with one's divine supply. Don't expect it to be easy. Practice makes perfect. And you will stumble and fall into old ways of thinking and feeling, but hold the new belief long enough and soon you and the page will be masters of the floating pentacle.

The Princess of Pentacles doesn't mind getting her hands dirty and perhaps could train you in the art of mudpie making or sandcastle building. Do you remember the last time you played in the sand at the beach? Or the last time you put your hands in the soil?

The Child of Earth is a great card to work with when you are starting to feel disengaged or disconnected from the world around you. We all feel this way from time to time, and it happens because we have stopped checking in with the energy from which we came, the earth. We become over-whelmed, sluggish, unmotivated, and stuck. Yet by using this card as an archetype, we can align ourselves easier with the basic yet necessary pulse of the earth. One way this can be done is by the very food we put in our mouths.

Have you ever grown your own food? The princess and the page both represent the small shoots of potential we all have. Not fully actualized and with a lot of growing to do, the Child of Earth shows us that we all take time to grow. The apple and the rabbit in the Gaian Tarot card allude to this very fact. Inside the apple is all you need to grow more apples, the seeds. The rabbit shows the fertile, rich condi-tions this potential truly has. Funny how we often forget that all we need is right inside of us as well. The fastest way to reconnect with this energy is to start a garden or at least maybe see if you can grow one food-giving plant.

The very act of digging in the soil and tending to a living breathing plant is a spiritual practice. And gardening is a very long-established active meditation process. You don't even have to have your own personal garden. Perhaps you can join a local garden project or maybe even volunteer for a larger commu-nity garden. More and more urban gardens are making their way into suburbs and the neighborhoods of overcrowded cities, showing us that the Princess of Pentacles spreads her influence and magic far and wide. Considering she is training to become the manifestation queen in the land of pentacles, it is a good sign that her training is headed in the right direction.

As a messenger

Page—The small Page of Pentacles would have a lot to report as he is in training to be a squire, the next step in his quest to be a knight. He is constantly learning and his days are filled with lessons. Let's think about what sort of lessons the Page of Pentacles might have to learn. One of his tasks may very well be keeping a journal or log book of all of the available resources of the kingdom. He may spend his day counting and tracking incomings and outgoings of food, livestock, clothes, and money. He may even be assigned to the outside of the castle to keep record of the physical structure of the walls that surround and protect the kingdom itself. One can conclude that at the end of the day, this page would have a lot to report. In fact, he would have the most up-to-date information about the kingdom's supply. This is a message that would be worth hearing as it is important for all of us to know what resources we have at our fingertips and which ones are getting dangerously low.

Because he is still learning, there is a good chance that this page has checked his facts and figures a couple of times before putting his final report together. The real lesson here is that if a page who would normally only be eight to twelve years old can be taught to keep these sorts of simple log books and journals, so can you. This page can bring an important message to be more watchful about what you have, where it is coming from, and how it is flowing out. This is a very simple first step in a much more complicated system, but some people miss simple altogether.

Princess—The Princess of Pentacles says it's time to get back to the earth. Crouch down low and listen with the soles of your feet instead of your ears. What do you feel? What can you hear?

Allow yourself to walk barefoot wherever possible so you can bring energy up from mother earth, all the while letting go of all static and unwanted energy that your physical body has collected. Did you know that walking barefoot on the grass is one of the best ways to rid the physical body of electrical energy? These days we are all full of it. Everything we touch has a charge to it, which makes letting it go even more important to our overall health and well being, as we were never designed to be fully loaded with electrical currents.

If the Princess of Pentacles has shown up in a reading, she very well could be asking you to unplug yourself, at least for a little while. Once upon a time, asking someone to unplug themselves would have sounded like lunacy as there would have been no need to deliberately go out of your way to work with the energy of the earth. Today is a different story. These days we need to schedule time to do things that were once a natural part of our lives. So take notice when the princess comes along, as she may be very well letting you know it is time to get back to your natural, primal ways of being.

Page of Swords: Child of Air

He who learns but does not think is lost. He who
thinks but does not learn is in great danger.
CONFUCIUS

Personification of Air
Zodiac Signs: Gemini, Libra, Aquarius
Keywords: Investigation, awareness, examination

As a person

Page—Young, childlike, and in many ways innocent, the Page
of Swords is not at all prepared to go into any sort of battle.
Just like a child is not equipped to make adult decisions, the
Page of Swords lacks the skills of the knight, queen, and king.
These distinctions are important as it can often seem like a

Page of Swords child is knowledgeable beyond his or her years. Eager to learn and full of questions, the Page of Swords can come across a lot more mature than numerical age implies. But don't let this fool you, as this young child is still driving with their training wheels on.

This page can still contribute, but there is a lack of some necessary skills required in a specific situation, circumstance, or goal. Listen carefully when the Page of Swords speaks, as their questions are often filled with bits of wonderful wisdom. Be aware enough to know that the question is seeking an answer that you may yourself have to provide. If you have ever been around a small child, you know they ask a lot of questions. In fact, they question pretty much everything. The word "why" is the most popular word in their vocabulary. Yet for whatever reason, that changes as we grow. We lose our need to learn and replace it with a false sense of knowing. This page has a lot to teach us about humility.

Reading, writing, and talking are personality traits of the Page of Swords. If you don't have children of your own, go see a close friend or family member who will let you "borrow" their three-to-six-year-old sometime. Notice how this child interacts with the world. Keep pen and paper ready, because the questions, observations, and statements you hear will be worth their weight in gold, or "out of the mouths of babes," as they say.

Princess—The Princess of Swords is always looking for the most logical and rational explanation of the world around her. She is an avid researcher and may be found in the middle of a pile of books. Not one to just take others' word for it, this princess sets about finding her own truth. In fact, truth and transparency are important to her, though sometimes it can be difficult to sort fact from fiction, especially if the truth defies logical explanation.

The Princess of Swords is more of a seeker in many ways. She wants to know things and is more than likely not to give up until she has explored all of her options. Sounds more like a little knight in training, doesn't it? The truth is, as queen she will need to be educated in both courtly and worldly matters. Her mind will end up being her most treasured weapon, which is why she is doing her very best to sharpen it now. The Princess of Swords is studious and possibly a geeky nerd, but she doesn't care. For she knows that her future self will thank her for all the mental training she is doing now.

As an archetypal influence

Page—The Page of Swords is the closest to a little knight as we get among the page cards. In Llewellyn's Classic Tarot, we see him practicing his skills, trying to look as grown up as possible, even though we all know he has a long way to go before the sword he holds in his hand will ever belong to him. I mean let's face it, he hasn't even made it to squire yet. Chances are he only got his hands on that sword when no one was looking or around to supervise him. It is the squire's duty to clean, polish, and shine the knight's armor and weapons, not the page. More than likely, this young page was charged with organizing the gear, readying it for his commanding squire. Practice makes perfect, right?

Just like the blade feels heavy in the page's hands, your thoughts, worries, and concerns may seem heavy when this card makes its way into a reading. It may also indicate that you need to seek guidance around your question from someone with more experience than you currently have. Sure, the page may be having a lot of fun waving around that sword, but he could seriously injure himself or someone else with his reckless, untrained actions. There is a reason young knights are trained with wooden swords first. Only when they have learned enough skill can they be armed with a battle weapon. Then and only then are they trained for combat. Not being ready for training is a key component of this card.

The Child of Air is practicing with all of his might just to keep that sword up off the ground. Keep in mind that swords are very heavy and it takes time, effort, and daily practice to learn to swing one of those prized metal blades. It's good advice for most of us, especially considering that swords represent the mind, thoughts, and mental agility, as it does take time, commitment, and daily practice to master one's mental faculties. Just like this young page, this card lets you know you need to get back to learning mode. It may be time to retrain your brain, or form a new habit, or even relearn how to make decisions with confidence and clarity.

Princess—Technically the Page of Swords in the Tarot of the Hidden Realm is not a princess, yet she sure does seem to embody Princess of Swords energy. I am not trying to gender this card, even though it looks like I am, but the reality is the princess as an archetype has very strong feminine energy, and it is this energy that is her point of attraction. For this reason we will be referring to her as if she is gendered female. Unlike the page we saw in Llewellyn's Classic Tarot, the sword's weight is a real issue for our princess warrior.

In the hands of the princess, this weight is also symbolic of the responsibilities to come once she steps into a larger position in her clan, be it as queen or head of her own royal army. This makes her practice even more important.

Can you see the focus she has? Her mind is squarely on learning her lessons. Unlike the Page of Swords, who does not seem to yet fully comprehend the meaning of his sword, the princess is determined to become one with the weapon she currently holds uneasily in her hands.

So why am I so adamant that this is actually a princess? Her hairpiece. The feather arrangement gives it away, as elaborate headdresses like this are only ever assigned to royalty or high ranking court/clan officials. Even the way Barbara Moore writes about this card hints at this young girl's special future potential. In her words, "Motivated not by praise or admiration from others, she wishes to be skilled ... Mastery over her craft, over herself, will give her the freedom to move through life with confidence, with the ability to do and achieve whatever she desires." Sure sounds like the making of a queen to me!

As a spiritual Influence

Page—Questioning is a skill, and the Page of Swords is learning it daily. Children don't seem to have a problem opening their mouths and asking for things. They don't even care if what they want sounds ridiculous and outlandish. They ask regardless of a response. Asking is important, for if you don't ask, you don't receive. The Page of Swords connects you to the inner child who asked for things they did and did not receive. Sometimes the asking was rewarded and sometimes it was not. For those who asked and did not receive, it is more than likely at some point the asking stopped. And once you stop asking, it becomes hard to start again, meaning that asking for help becomes so painful you prefer not to ask at all.

The Child of Air in the Gaian Tarot shows us that sometimes we don't even have to open our mouths to ask—we simple need to put out our hand. The Child of Air could not verbally ask the butterfly to land on her hand, but the very action of just holding it out signaled the child's receptive nature. Being able to give and receive is a spiritual practice. Asking and listening are also spiritual pursuits.

The Page of Swords can assist you in learning how to ask for what you require. They can teach you how to question and how to stop and listen to the answers you seek. Listening is crucial if you really want to refine your asking technique. For the next week, keep track of all the questions that pop into your head. Write them down, speak them aloud, and just see what happens. Set a question as a point of meditation and then spend the rest of your meditation time being open and receptive to the answer. Keep the Page of Swords near you as you meditate so it can act as guide, mentor, and spiritual ally.

Princess—In spiritual practice, the step that most people miss is the smallest and it's the first step you take after you figure out where you are beginning from. Everyone wants the awakening right now! Yet this form of awareness happens over time, and you start fresh each and every time you sit your butt down and take a nice deep breath. When I was learning how to meditate, I would get so annoyed by the fact that I could not sit still for hours and hours on end. Voices kept invading my mental space and I could never seem to reach that wonderful space of nothingness inside my own head. I was about to stop trying when finally I had a breakthrough: my mind was not fit enough for what I was trying to make it do. It was instead flabby and weak—and that was more than okay. At least I had a starting point. Once you have a firm starting point, your finish line doesn't look quite so far away.

The Princess of Swords reminds you that the mind is just like the body. You can't expect to run a marathon if you can't even run past the end of your driveway. But you can train and build the muscles to endure lengthier bouts of work and strain. You can also train your mind to be calm, quiet, and still. You just have to take it one small step at a time.

Start with something attainable. I get my students to start with mastering two minutes before they try five. Hold a thought, vision, or goal in your mind for just two minutes. See if you can do so without interference from other invading thoughts. Try meditating for only two minutes. Hold a yoga pose or mudra for only two minutes. Or chant for only two minutes. Become the two-minute master of the mind. You may not think this will achieve much, but the Princess of Swords knows that this simple step is the difference between staying forever a princess or becoming a queen.

As a messenger

Page—Pages really are a great reminder that we don't need to go it alone; oftentimes it's not in our best interest. As a messenger, the page asks you to seek council or guidance. Now would be a very good time to speak to a coach, mentor, or elder about what you are thinking or wanting to try, do, or pull off. This does not at all mean that your idea, thought, or belief is wrong or bad; it is more to make sure you have the right sort of structure and form necessary for your ideas to bring you the results you seek. Whether or not your idea is good or bad will more than likely be indicated by the cards surrounding your Page of Swords in a reading. That said, it is liberating to know that it really doesn't matter how things turn out, as you are just like the page: still learning. Failure is not only expected but encouraged. All we can really hope for is that you put that bloody big sword down before you cut someone's head off!

Like all children, our little Page of Swords really just wants to have fun.

So how are you having fun with your ideas? Are you thinking big enough? Are you truly allowing that imaginative unlimited creative mind of the child to filter through, or are you taking yourself way too seriously? Maybe the page has shown up to cut you some slack.

When a page shows up in a reading, people can feel ready to take on the world, but the truth is they won't pull off those wild crazy plans unless they have someone with more knowledge backing them up. That sword in his hands is pretty sharp, so if slack or release is what you need, go ahead and cut those cords holding you down. Just be mindful that this kid is not exactly a pro at swinging that thing, so keep your fingers and toes safely protected.

Princess—Unlike the page, the Princess of Swords is working on filling her queenly shoes. She may only be in training right now but she knows that learning to make decisions effectively is a skill that can be learned at any age. The princess will more than likely make more than her fair share of misguided and impulsive decisions, but that's okay for now. As I said before, we need to fail in order to refine our skills.

Getting it wrong now means getting it right later. Trial and error are what this princess is all about. Yet the biggest lesson of all is learning how to make any decision the right decision. One of the best ways to eliminate fear and doubt is to just go ahead and make a decision and then work at making it the right decision, even if it doesn't work out or blows up in your face. When this princess shows up in a reading, know that you are being asked how you can make your decision the right one, regardless of the outcome.

Page of Cups: Child of Water

*Let us not forget that the little emotions are the great
captains of our lives and we obey them without realizing it.*
Vincent Van Gogh

Personification of Water
Zodiac signs: Cancer, Scorpio, Pisces
Keywords: Sensitivity, moody, artistic

As a person

Page—Of all the tarot pages, the Page of Cups is the most sensitive. He is emotional, creative, and intuitive, causing him to become overwhelmed from time to time. The Page of Cups has an affinity for water and may often be referred to as a "water baby" because he is always in it, as illustrated by the

Child of Water card in the Gaian Tarot. Water is where this young page feels most at home. The noise of the waves and the roar of the surf comfort this young child like nothing else. If they could, these children would never leave the beach.

This young page feels his way through the world, relying more on his gut and inner vision than logic and reason. This is not to say he can't use both; it's just that he will always go with how he feels first. This makes the Page of Cups personality more of an emotional learner. In other words, they need to be able to make a deep connection to what they are learning. They need to feel that it is relevant and safe for them to open themselves up and receive its lessons and guidance.

Because this child of water is so caught up in his emotional world, these types of children can seem standoffish or even self-absorbed. This is not because they do not care about those around them, quite the opposite really. It is more that they feel so deeply that they often get lost and swept away in the emotional energy that other people bring to their world. Page of Cups personalities often take on the moods and personality traits of those who come into their circle of influence, which is why it is so important to teach these water babies how to deal with and protect their emotional bodies.

Princess—If ever there were a perfect real-life example of the Princess of Cups, it would be Princess Diana of Wales. Although at the time of her death she was known as the "queen of hearts," the reality is that she was only a princess. But who she was and how she chose to wear her label of princess is important. To be honest, I have no idea just how much influence Diana had on the United States of America and its culture, but in Australia she was a very prominent feature of my formative years. Her grace, beauty, pain, and heart were everywhere.

Unlike the page, the princess does not get time to play, explore, or even talk to fish. The page and the Princess of Cups are both in training but for very different roles. This is very important when you get the Princess of Cups in a reading instead of the Page of Cups. Sure, they might both be young and inexperienced, learning as they go with many things to master, but only the princess will have to give up her playful, self-indulgent ways and replace them with duty and obedience.

As an archetypal influence

Page—In many respects, this card is an archetype for childhood memories. No matter if you remember them as good or bad, it's really about *how* you remember them—keeping in mind that memories are a tricky thing. All our memories are seen through the emotional charge that created them, which is why two people very rarely remember the same moment in their past the same way. If you have a large family, you will know exactly what I mean. You may remember magic moments on summer vacations, yet your siblings only remember being bored out of their minds.

When this page shows up in a reading, he really wants you to revisit something from your childhood. So take a short walk down memory lane and explore some of the memories you created between the ages of eight and twelve.

Where did you live when you were that age?

What school did you go to? Were you popular or a wallflower? What did you think of yourself at that age, and were the opinions of others important to you? What was your favorite TV show, food, sport, book? Now consider if any of this matters at all to you today. Oftentimes when this page shows up in a reading, he is a key to unlocking, healing, or clearing a childhood habit, belief, or behavioral pattern. Really think if there is anything from this part of your life that is relevant or significant for where you now find yourself.

Do you have similar feelings, people, or situations in your life that once again need addressing?

Princess—As an archetype, the Princess of Cups shows the dichotomy of duty and personal responsibility. Princess Diana's sense of duty always outweighed her personal need for peace, privacy, and solitude. The young princess learns very early in her role that her own personal needs are of little or no consequence. The Princess of Cups lives deep inside her emotional center, meaning she feels more of this loss and strain than the other three princesses. If she does not learn to master this watery world, it will leave her vulnerable and at the mercy of the rising tides.

When the Princess of Cups is out of power or reversed, she becomes prone to depression; the worst part is that those around her will often miss it. They will instead mistake her smiling face and social graces for enjoyment. They will continue to inflict pain upon her with loose tongues and flippant remarks. She may even find herself being told over and over again to toughen up and grow a thicker skin. Those around the Princess of Cups often mistake her pain for boredom and will then be surprised when this incredible spirit eventually drowns.

Young girls drowning themselves in sex, booze, and drugs show classic out-of-power Princess of Cups energy. They have yet to learn how to deal with all they feel, sense, and take in. Being numb is just so much easier. Perhaps you know someone who fits this description, or you your-self may have lived through Princess of Cups phases in your life. I know I have. As a highly sensitive introvert, numbness was my BFF. How nice to know that we can turn this energy around and grow into very capable queens.

As a spiritual influence

Page—In Llewellyn's Classic Tarot, we see our little Page of Cups standing near the shoreline gazing at the fish in his cup. The fish has its mouth open, and to be honest it is hard to figure out if the fish is talking to the page or gasping for air. Of all the pages, this is the only one consistently shown with an animal totem, a fish. This page seems to have a con-stant traveling companion. But what role does the little fish play in this card? Is it the page's master/teacher/mentor? Or is the fish that seems to reside inside his cup his conscience, like Jimminy Cricket but in fish form?

One thing we do know for sure is that this fish needs water; he doesn't breathe air like his human companion. Fish need water to live, so even though he may appear perched over the lip of our little page's cup, his ability to surface for an extended period of time is limited. Much like how the Page of Cups won't be in his station for very long, his cur-rent state of being is also temporary.

Water truly is necessary for all life. Without it, nothing lives—not us, the fish, or the page. We all come from the water, hence this card often being linked to pregnancy. It has strong second chakra energy to it, and there is no doubt that when one is working with this card, one is also working with their sacral chakra, the watery energy center out of which all is born. This energy center also stores emotional memory. Maybe the fish is a memory from childhood. Perhaps the Page of Cups is asking us to look at one or more of our childhood memories and see if they are supporting and nurturing us, or trying to pull us under and drown us. This could be why the page in Llewellyn's Classic Tarot is looking at the fish with so much skepticism.

Princess—In the Tarot of the Hidden Realm, we see a young girl gazing into a silver cup. Her gaze is relaxed yet focused, and we have to wonder: what exactly does she see in there? There is a good chance this young lady is practicing her scrying lessons. Water has been used since ancient times for the divination practice of scrying—that is, looking into a reflective surface to seek an answer or clues about the coming future.

With her deep connection to water, it is not unreasonable to presume that the Princess of Cups would be a good study buddy if you want to expand your divination skills. Gazing into water is a skill that takes a lot of time and patience. Oh, and did I mention it can be extremely boring? This form of intuitive learning is not for those who have trouble sitting still. You need to be able to hold your cup calmly in your hands and see past your own reflection in the water.

Being able to see what is beyond the surface is important. Far too often people get stuck on what they perceive to be the only thing in their field of vision. Yet this princess is learning that in order to really see what is going on, you have to see beyond the reflection, or should I say projection. Seeing with your inner vision is not the same as seeing with your physical vision. It is up to you to train your eyes to see both. Eventually the Princess of Cups will be just as skilled as the queen, but for now she must stay alert and practice her deep water gazing.

As a messenger

Page—Fish live in water, and it is crucial to their survival, meaning they can also tell if the water is clean, dirty, safe, or hazardous. Fish know when to go with the current and when to get out of its way. Water also represents emotions. In fact, our human emotional energy center is connected to the element of water. Perhaps this fish is instructing our sensitive child on how to navigate his emotional waters. Maybe it offers some encouragement and tips on how to use his emotional energy to his benefit and not allow it to become his weak point.

Just like the watery Page of Cups, your emotions would have run high at this age. You too would have been learning a lot about your world, your family, and your place in all of it. Ages eight to twelve is a time when children start to form their own opinions of the world and what they believe to be right and wrong. This can and does cause conflict with the adult self that now finds itself living in the world the page once imagined. If you have this sort of conflict going on in your life and the Page of Cups shows up in a reading, know it is now time to figure out if you are really seeing what's there or if you are seeing your life through the lens of the emotional child.

Clear vision may be needed at this time. Stop moving around and stand still for the moment so you can get a clearer picture of what is actually going on.

Princess—The Princess of Cups tends to get swallowed up and spat out by the very world that needs her the most. This is something to keep in mind if she shows up in a reading.

Do the cards around her support her? Or are they looking to destroy her?

We need more personalities like hers in our world. More than ever, we need them to teach us how to open our hearts, allow ourselves to be vulnerable, and guide us to the depths of our emotional centers. This card can offer you an incredible gift but it can also give you a weighty burden.

The Princess of Cups can bless you with a deep heart connection to another person, idea, or situation. She can show you how to express yourself freely and can even train you in the ways of social duty, or in other words, how to get yourself invited to all the right events, parties, and conferences. Bear in mind that she will bring with her discomfort, sensitivity, and more often than not, the feeling of being overwhelmed.

Page of Wands: Child of Fire

I have no special talents. I am only passionately curious.
ALBERT EINSTEIN

Personification of Fire
Zodiac signs: Aries, Leo, Sagittarius
Keywords: Enthusiasm, curiosity, impetuous

As a person

Page—The Page of Wands is a bit of a trickster. Not one to stand still for too long, this young page is always looking for ways to keep energy moving. The Child of Fire is always on the go and can be quite exhausting to deal with if you yourself are not programed for this sort of constant activity. I often think children who are diagnosed with ADHD are Page of Wands personalities, as the Page of Wands gets bored very, very quickly. I don't make this claim flippantly, as I grew up with a sibling with ADHD who by the way was never medicated.

These types of children like to be on the move all the time, both in body and mind, much like the young boy on the Page of Wands card in the Tarot of the Hidden Realm. He looks like he is mischief just waiting to happen. Burning hot and full of passion, the Page of Wands is just as likely to beat you over the head with his big stick as he is to build some interesting wooden contraption with it. To say this particular page is reactive may be an understatement.

In many respects, this card could very well represent a young boy with his first sexual erection—also known as wood. His desires are ignited but he is unsure what to do with it. It might explain why he has to hold it with two hands. It is said that when stimulated, our sexual energy center feels hot, like it is burning, hence the term "burning desire." This arousal is the spark that lights the flame, and this young page is just starting to learn how to deal with sparks, fire, and wood.

In much the same way we learn that personal desire is not a toy, fire, sparks, and flames also need respect and honor. If we allow our desires to rule us, they will ruin us just as quickly as any fire could. The Page of Wands needs to find ways to control his flames.

Princess—Just as the Page of Wands can represent the onset of male puberty, the Princess of Wands can represent the onset of female puberty, something not everyone is comfortable discussing. Young girls feel desire just as strongly as young boys, and it consumes just as much of their time as it does for their male counterparts. The difference is that young girls master it a lot more quickly.

If you have a pubescent daughter and this card keeps coming up for you in a reading, it may very well be telling you she needs to talk. Even if you are not the person she wishes to speak with, she may very well need someone to talk with about what is going on with her body. She may need to be walked through her sudden introduction to desire. Desire itself is not a bad thing, but when it becomes the only energy we deal with, it can become distorted and destructive.

As an archetypal influence

Page—Have you ever looked at a classical version of the Page of Wands card closely and wondered what the heck this page is staring at on his stick? Maybe it's just me, but I notice these things.

No matter how many times I look at the Page of Wands from Llewellyn's Classic Tarot, I can't help but wonder what is running through this little page's mind, especially considering he holds his stick (wand) firmly with both hands.

Is he about to break out into some kick-ass moves? Is he just contemplating the combustible nature of this piece of wood he now grips in his clutches? If it were to self-combust, then what?

Perhaps this is why our young page always seems to be shown with the salamander on his tunic. The salamander needs water; in fact, it cannot live without moist skin.

Water is an important controlling element of fire. Unlike the Page of Cups and his fish, the Page of Wands never seems to actually interact with the salamander. It just appears on his clothing like a family crest or a reminder of how to handle the very element in which he is being schooled.

As an archetype, the Page of Wands shows us that not everyone who handles fire knows what they are doing with it. All fire eaters need to start somewhere, even if "safety measures" means keeping a bucket of water handy in case things go horribly wrong. Despite the risks involved in his training, this page is not putting that stick down anytime soon. Passion is like that. It draws you in and keeps you locked in its vortex until you find a way to take control of the situation.

Princess—Much like the Princess of Swords seems more warrior than princess, so too does the Princess of Wands. Curious and hungry for knowledge, this princess suffers from a condition known as "ants in the pants"—or in this princess's case, "fire ants in the pants"! The Princess of Wands has an adventurous spirit, and much like the blazing energy of her element, sitting still and staying in one place for too long doesn't really seem to be her thing.

Wands is the suit of action, movement, desire, and passion and this little princess is all hopped up on the high octane vibe of this energy. You won't find her loafing around eating cake and ice cream and watching Netflix. Instead you will find her where the action is. Wherever the energy is high, this princess will gravitate toward it.

This may explain why this card often depicts a young woman learning archery, kendo, or some other form of physical stick-related combat. Like her young male counterpart the page, she needs to find something to do with all that newfound heat. If this princess has found her way into your reading or daily draw, she may be telling you it's time to get off your butt. Alternatively, she may be showing you how to actively deal with all that pent-up energy. Either way, you can be assured that you are going to be moving your body somewhere sometime soon.

As a spiritual influence

Page—Many years ago when I was learning tarot, I heard someone talk about how they saw the suit of wands as real magic wands, and the spark or flame they represented was divine magic itself. I loved this from the first moment I heard it; here with the page, it brings other things to ponder.

If we take a look at the Page of Wands from Llewellyn's Classic Tarot, we notice that the page's stick seems to be alive. How curious, especially as we know good and well that a branch of a tree cannot continue to live once it has been severed from its host. But if it is magic, containing its own life force energy and in the charge of our young page, his level of responsibility just increased. Now we can somewhat empathize with his enjoyment—how exciting it must be to stand at the threshold of magical training!

What would you do if you were given a real magical wand just for a day?

Would you be ready to launch into your lessons despite the very real risk of everything blowing up in your face? Or would you be too scared to even wave the wand around?

Let us not forget that the Page of Wands wields his fiery stick with his training wheels firmly attached. He does not have any real talent at this point; it really is all hit-or-miss. Even if there is a possibility here, it still could go either way. The other cards around the Page of Wands are important for this reason, as they will give you more of an understanding of which way the magic (the fire) is headed.

Let's say for example that the Page of Wands in a three-card reading is the last card. We could look at the cards that came before as products of the page's magic.

The Page of Wands's skill in spellcasting will depend on the nature of the cards. Put the Page of Wands in front of the other two cards, and we get a glimpse of what possible outcomes might be created if the person continues to wave his or her wand around without further training.

As with all the wands family, there is going to be risk involved in actions you take. But sometimes that action can bring you rewards beyond your wildest dreams. Keep learning to control your magic just like the page, and very soon you will be able to create anything and everything you could ever possibly need.

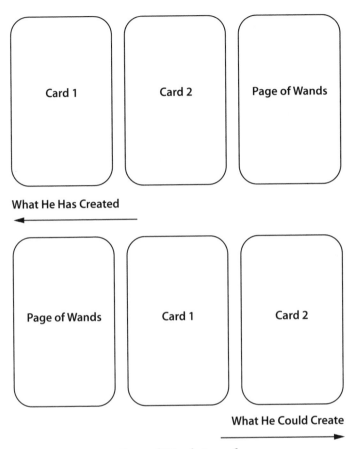

Page of Wands Spread

Princess—One of my favorite Princess of Wands images is from Emily Carding's Tarot of the Sidhe, which looks eerily similar to the Arrow Master card from Colette Baron-Reid's Wisdom of the Hidden Realms oracle. The reason I bring both of these up is because I love this particular archetype of the Princess of Wands as a markswoman in training. As queen, this princess will need to know how to act quickly, calmly, and without doubt. She will need to have mastered not only her element of fire but its force and power. And she will need to do all of this with confidence and conviction.

Learning archery seems only fitting, as it teaches one how to read conditions and surroundings. It also teaches how to aim for something correctly and offers schooling in patience and accuracy. And of course, let's not forget the level of detachment necessary to allow the arrow to play its part once released from the bowstring. What a perfect way for this young princess to channel all of that high-octane energy she now finds coursing through her body.

As a messenger

Page—The Child of Fire (Page of Wands) has a lot to learn, that is for sure. He needs to not only learn how to ignite his fire, but he also needs to learn how to control it so it does not destroy him. In the Gaian Tarot we see the sheer joy fire brings to this young child, but I can't help but wonder if he is playing with something he hasn't yet experienced the consequences of. In other words, I don't think he knows the "joy" of being burned.

Do you remember the very first time you burnt yourself on an open flame? In the household of my youth, we were taught the lessons of the physical world swiftly. And I have to say I am grateful, as knowing that fire burns, hurts, and brings pain humbles us. We come to terms with fire's destructive ways and learn that it is not a toy but a responsibility.

As a messenger, the Page of Wands could be telling you a few things—is it time to pick up your magic wand and start your magic lessons? It could also be telling you to be mindful of how your personal desires are surfacing. Desire in and of itself is not a bad thing, but when we allow our desires to dominate our time and energy, we will have a problem. There is also the possibility that this page could be telling you that things you have been working on have started to create a life force all their own. This is an important message, as tending to something already growing and nurturing something only beginning to grow are *very* different, requiring different energies. One takes a lot less energy than the other.

Princess—If you do not have a daughter and the Princess of Wands keeps appearing in a reading or daily draw, it may be time to take a look at your current set of desires.

Where is this new and exciting energy coming from, and where is it taking you or distracting you? Ask yourself, "What is my current point of attraction and where do I have my arrow aimed?" Be mindful that you are the princess and not the queen. You may have to check yourself a couple of times and be patient a little while longer before you release the tension and let the arrow soar. You may have to live with the fact that you might miss your mark a few times before hitting it. Just don't give up, as this is merely the beginning and there is much more to learn and much more to be discovered and devoured.

The Princess of Wands offers the opportunity to ride this pulsating electrifying wave. She says it's okay to take the ride and get on and enjoy, as long as you understand that the end result at this point is in no way guaranteed and at best it's a crap shoot. Other than that, it should get you going, just for a little while.

Connecting Exercises and Spreads

Whether we like to admit it or not, we all have things in life we don't really like to do. They are boring, mind-numbing, and often thankless. The good news is that most of the time these things are quick, simple, and don't require much of our time. Think about the life of our page, as his or her life is all of those mundane, monotonous things. For the page, however, the tasks are not quick or simple and can drag on for months, even years. The life of a page is an incredibly boring one.

Imagine being the "page of stairs" for a year, not doing anything other than taking the names of all those who went up and down the stairs. You'd be unable to leave your post to eat or use the bathroom unless someone remembered you were actually there. Yet somehow in those long tedious months and years, you would learn about patience, diligence, and everything about that household you now call home. From their passive and nonintrusive position, the pages became living, breathing information guides to the castle and the inner workings of the kingdom. All this from just doing the most simple and boring tasks.

This is the real lesson of the pages. To find the treasures in the mundane. The joy in the joyless and the wisdom in being invisible.

In order to truly understand this lesson, I recommend working with one page card for a thirty-day period. You can select it any way you want, be it consciously as you are already aware of what area you need to go back to basics with, or intuitively by placing the pages face down and selecting the one that feels aligned to your energy. There is no wrong or right way to select your card.

Once you have selected the page you are going to work with for the next thirty days, it is your job to become that page. Go through each day as that page would have been expected to. It is also your job to find as many creative and different ways to do the tasks your page would do. Let me give you an example.

I often work with the Page of Pentacles, as this card teaches me about my physical world more than most other cards in the tarot; the page is a detached observer, merely learning all he can so he can become squire. What happens to what he observes is irrelevant to his task: to watch, record, and not pass judgment.

In a thirty-day period with the Page of Pentacles, I keep track of spending, savings, eating habits, exercise, physical health, energy levels, and daily habits. All I do is keep a record, write it all down. At the end of the thirty days, I have a very clear picture of where I am doing well and what areas I have been neglecting. I can also pinpoint areas of resistance by seeing which of the above areas I was reluctant to increase my level of awareness of or did not record well.

So go ahead and select your page, step into his or her shoes, and let the learning begin!

Your Inner Child Spread

The page cards are perfect cards to work with when it comes to inner child work. Some of us have happy and joyful inner children, some do not. They can be wounded, angry, hurt, neglected, alone, or feel unloved. Inner child energy is very powerful and can be responsible for bad habits and self-destructive patterns of behavior. Our inner child can be the biggest gift we have *or* the temper-tantrum-throwing drama queen that stops us from expanding, growing, and having the life of our dreams. This spread will give you a little insight into how your inner child is working and what sort of energy currently surrounds it.

Take some time to think about which part of your inner child you wish to work with in this spread. Recall the selection techniques on the previous page. Take your page card and place it in the center of your spread as illustrated in the following diagram. Once your page is in place, shuffle your deck. Draw four more cards, placing them in the order illustrated in the diagram.

- *Card One*—This card represents the environment in which your inner child grew up. This is an important card, as it is not emotionally invested in your personal memories. It simply lets you know what energy surrounded you at the time your page archetype was developing.

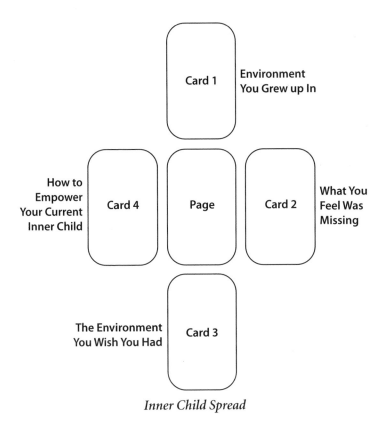

Inner Child Spread

- *Card Two*—This card represents what was missing while your page was growing. More to the point, it reveals what your inner child feels it missed out on. This card reveals wounds or issues that may still need some healing work.

- *Card Three*—This card represents what kind of environment your inner child craves. Note that this may not always be constructive energy, so please don't be dismayed if a not-so-friendly card shows up in this position.

In many ways, this card can shed light on self-destructive behaviors or inner triggers. If it is a positive and constructive card, that is fabulous. Above all, know that there is no wrong or right card in this position.

• *Card Four*—This card represents how best to harness your inner child energy moving forward. This card also gives you hints and clues for empowering your inner child if it feels shy or timid as well as how you might cool it off if it is somewhat reactive.

three

Knights and Princes

In essence, if we want to direct our lives, we must take control of our consistent actions. It's not what we do once in a while that shapes our lives, but what we do consistently.

TONY ROBBINS

. . . .

In this chapter, we will be exploring the four knights of the tarot court along with their alter egos, the four princes. Just so we are clear, a prince can be a knight but a knight cannot become a prince unless he somehow marries a princess or queen. I know it sounds like semantics for its own sake, but it is actually quite important when it comes to learning the very different roles these cards represent. As princes are often groomed for the throne, their end game is becoming king, but knights? Not so much. As you will see, these are not the only titles this particular archetype has, such as in the Gaian Tarot, where the knight is known as the explorer. This card can also represent the third stage in human development: adolescence or early adulthood. This energy is evident in many depictions of the knight and prince cards. Interestingly, "knight" as a job title persists even after reaching adulthood and middle age. When one becomes a knight, it is for life.

History, Myth, and Legend

Of all the positions in the royal court, the role of the knight is the most complex and diverse. When one first thinks of a knight, one automatically conjures the image of a medieval warrior covered in fabulously decorative plate armor, mounted on his noble steed, ready to defend his realm on the battlefield. Although it is true that the majority of medieval knights were a group of socially elite men who wore armor and fought atop horses, the definition of "knight" changed and evolved throughout history. In essence, this is only one version of what a knight was or could be. You see, not all knights went off into battle, nor did they dress in armor—some never even rode a horse. In the historical sense, knights had many different roles and served many different functions depending on their place within society and their political aspirations.

The socio-political position of the knight allowed knights to form their own class structure, which served to shape the evolution of knightly roles over the course of five centuries. Knights could be landowners with large estates. They could become and serve as an officer of the court, acting as judges, jurors, or commissioners. Evidence of their different roles and interests can be found in short stories and chronicles written by knights who considered themselves scribes and writers.

There are also many legal and religious documents showing how some knights pondered their role between church and country in a very political and philosophical way. It's not exactly the image of the bloodthirsty warrior, is it?

It is these complex personas of the knight we see in the four court cards. The land owner could very well be the Knight of Pentacles. The knight of justice and battle can be seen in the Knight of Swords. The lover, poet, and writer is more than evident in the Knight of Cups, and the knight of action, adventure, and passion is represented by the Knight of Wands. Of course there's much more to our four knights than this; more will be discussed in their own separate sections. But I want you to understand where these knightly archetypes came from. I want you to feel some connection to the deep history and legacy of the real-life knights who influenced the four knights of the tarot, as this will only deepen your relationship with these four cards.

Despite the many different roles and obligations the knights had, they did have one thing in common—the ritual of becoming a knight. In order to become a knight in the first place, one needed to be dubbed, knighted, or belted. This was the easy part, and for knights who lived their lives in title only, this was pretty much the *only* part. For the rest of the medieval knights, however, the next phase was the most challenging of all: training and skill development. Training for a knight was not a one-time thing that stopped once basic skills were mastered. Training for a knight was a lifelong affair.

Habits started long before a knight actually became a knight; they began when he was a squire, the position our pages are in training for. Squires work under a knight as an apprentice. In this position they learn how to act, dress, and conduct themselves as knights. They also learn about the care and expertise regarding their armor, weapons, and horses. The first skill that all knights need to learn is horsemanship. Regardless of how one becomes a knight, these skills are required, even for princes who take up the sword. Princes, however, never leave the home to undertake training as it is just too dangerous to leave the safety and protection of the court.

The horse and the knight are inseparable. Yet a knight has more than one horse. Unlike the romantic versions of knights that TV and film have created, the knight did not just have one faithful horse companion. Knights had to have many horses for many different purposes. Knights had horses for war and battle, horses trained to take place in tournaments, and horses specifically trained for royal parades. Each horse also had to be fitted with the appropriate armor, leather, and decorative headdress. The more horses a knight had in his caravan, the higher his social status.

By the end of the sixteenth century, the power of the knights had all but faded, their roles amounting to nothing more than a title and a handshake. As Sir John Cleese has been noted for saying, being a knight in the twenty-first century won't even get you out of a parking ticket! Yet five hundred years of knightly history is more than long enough to embed the knight into our cellular memory and collective consciousness. As you make your way through the four knights of the tarot court, honor the history and legacy they represent. Understand the lifelong commitment to excellence each of them has made, and never underestimate their power.

Knight of Pentacles: Explorer of Earth

Abundance is not something we acquire.
It is something we tune into.
Wayne Dyer

Mutable Earth
Zodiac sign: Virgo
Keywords: Discerning, methodical, responsible

As a person

Knight—The Knight of Pentacles is somewhat of a homebody. He is much more content to stay close to his kingdom than run off into the great unknown. This one personality trait separates him from the other three knights. It's probably just as well, as not all knights are meant to traipse off into battle or ride off into the sunset. These knights protect the castle grounds and all those who live within its walls. That's lucky for our Knight of Pentacles, because he finds shoring up boundaries and keeping track of what comes in and what goes out of the castle the most important of tasks. Accordingly, he does not take them lightly. Look at how focused and steady the Knight of Pentacles is in Llewellyn's Classic Tarot. He is fully present and aware of his task. Nothing could be more important to this knight than what he is doing right now. His slow, steady approach to life makes him the perfect candidate for his role as castle knight.

It takes real confidence to take one's time, to let things grow and evolve naturally and on their own terms. This confidence can be mistaken for stubbornness, for once the knight has made up his mind or decided on his course of action, it is almost impossible to sway him. For the Knight of Pentacles, each and every step taken is deliberate and worthy. How many of us can say that in a world of constant busyness? This knight has the ability to slow things down, to apply the brakes and make sure all the boxes have been ticked and all possible outcomes have been examined.

You won't be able to rush this knight, so don't bother. He will get it done when he gets it done. Fans of *A Song of Ice and Fire*, the popular fantasy series, could look at its author, George R. R. Martin, in this light. He is in no hurry to get the last books in the series written. He has even missed two contractual deadlines, yet the books themselves seem to be nowhere in sight. He is taking his time, making sure each and every word counts. He won't be rushed. And as a fan myself, I know waiting for this Knight of Pentacles will be well worth the wait.

Prince—Kings need to know diplomacy and strategy. They also need to know how to apply it to their own court and kingdom. The Prince of Pentacles is the King of Pentacles in training. He must now embark on the same lessons his father took before him, like knowing what resources he has at his disposal at any given time or knowing his kingdom's strengths and weak points. These lessons may not be the most glamorous at times, but they are vitally important. Sometimes the only way to learn these lessons is firsthand. Walking or riding the kingdom's boundaries each and every day is one way of knowing what is normal and what is not, or what is in its proper place and what is not.

Taking time and practicing the art of observation may not seem very exciting, but the truth is that the Prince of Pentacles could not think of a better way to spend his time. Getting down and dirty with his lessons is his personal learning style. He likes to learn on the job and out in the field. People with Prince of Pentacles energy will be very similar, preferring to be more hands-on and shown things again and again. This prince is thus very methodical.

Think about someone who has to learn the workings of their family's company from the mail room up. They would have a much better understanding of all the working parts and process than someone who went from business school to boardroom. John Bolinder is a fine example of this very energy. He started his career in the mail room of Nelson Labs before making his way up to CFO. So it makes sense that if this young prince is to best know and understand his kingdom and follow in his father's footsteps, he needs to do so one step at a time.

As an archetypal influence

Knight—I have often thought that the Knight of Pentacles is a great archetype for introverts like myself. There are some weeks I don't leave my house at all, and it's not because I fear the outside world or wish I wasn't in it—quite the opposite. I have everything I need right where I am. I know every square inch of my home and land intimately. There is always something to do at home, and here in my very introverted sanctuary, peace and harmony reign supreme. To be honest, it is because of this safety net that I deal so well with the world around me. When coming from a calm, peaceful, grounded place like the Knight of Pentacles, the world outside always looks brighter.

Note how comfortable the Explorer of Earth in the Gaian Tarot looks—close to the earth and more comfortable on the ground. This knight is a fabulous pin-up for introverts everywhere. Without anyone or anything to distract her, she is quite content to learn the lesson of where she is. Unafraid to be with her own thoughts and feelings, the Explorer of Earth finds solace in her lush surroundings. And it is not like she is perfectly alone anyway, as the forest itself provides an endless parade of friends to come by and say hello, like the deer and badger in the card.

When this card shows up in a reading or daily draw, you very well could find yourself needing to withdraw for a while. It may very well be time to start paying attention to your home and the environment you have created for yourself.

Is it safe? Does it provide you with everything you require? Where are its weak spots? How can you use the energy of the

Knight of Pentacles to slow things down so you can be more methodical?

These are not always easy questions to answer, so allow the knight to guide you one step at a time. When you and he have completed the step you are on, move on to the next.

Prince—Many people don't understand what "process" really means. You hear people say "I am going to be writer," or "I am going to be an entrepreneur," but they don't really understand the process that must be followed to achieve the titles they want to be able to claim. What most people really mean is, "I want to be famous and I want money to fall from the sky without me actually having to do anything for it." Unfortunately, it just doesn't work that way…and no one knows this better than the Prince of Pentacles.

The Prince of Pentacles is also aware enough to know that in order to be successful as a king, he is going to need some help. With the Prince of Pentacles as your archetype, you can be assured that you will feel the pull to learn more and you will even be prodded to find teachers to show you exactly how to do the things you need to do. A process is much easier to learn when you have someone to assist you in navigating the steps. The prince is not afraid to seek instruction and neither should you be. If you don't know how to do something, find someone who does. If you really want to be a writer but have no idea what that actually means in the real world, find a professional writer and ask them. Join online writing groups. Go to writers' conferences and learn all you can about the process of writing and being a writer. If you truly want to try your hand at becoming an entrepreneur, then find some entrepreneurs and study under them.

Remember that this prince is hands-on, so he won't be able to learn as effectively as he needs to if he is not in a position to physically explore the ideas and concepts that are being taught to him. This is important for you also as you truly start your journey, the process you must undergo in order to win the crown you wish to wear on your head.

As a spiritual influence

Knight—The Knight of Pentacles in the Tarot of the Hidden Realm is barefoot and close to the ground, as he seeks resources in the environment around him. He uses simple twigs to construct a five-pointed star. The twigs are not fixed or fastened together, however; in fact, he is still studying the piece he's working on. The unfinished star can still change, expand, or even fall apart at the last minute.

This slow, curious energy would be enough to drive some people bonkers. In a world of instant everything, the Knight of Pentacles becomes a difficult energy to work with. Yet this energy is vitally important in all spiritual practices. Prayer, meditation, and ritual all take time. They have very specific steps and procedures to follow and all need to be done in a very specific order. This means slowing down and taking time to make sure there are no missed steps along the way.

When we start a spiritual journey, we need to understand that it is not going to be fulfilled in a single weekend at a retreat. The retreat may be a fantastic starting point, but that's all it is. A spiritual journey is a lifelong commitment, much like becoming a knight. It takes time, consistent practice, dedication, and willingness to be in it for the long haul, no matter what happens along the path. This is the energy of the Knight of Pentacles. He is in it for the long haul, which is why he is more than willing to give his current task of building a star with twigs as much attention as it requires. And when he is finished, he will more than likely leave the twigs on the ground so they continue on their own spiritual path of rebirth.

When this knight shows up in a reading or daily draw, your commitment levels may be called into question. Are you showing up and giving all of yourself to your tasks? Are you fully present and aware in your relationships? What areas of your life are you committed to for the long haul?

Use these questions as points of meditation. Do not allow yourself to randomly or half-heartedly answer them. Sit with them and allow them to come to you on their own time, on their own terms. When you slow down enough to do this, you will be surprised at the answers that reveal themselves.

Prince—If you could be a prince of one thing in the material world, what would it be? Think about it carefully. The Prince of Pentacles offers you an opportunity to govern elements of your physical world. So what will it be? Health? Money? Food? Shelter? Transportation? Something else? To be king you need to learn and master them all, but here in the shoes of the prince you can take them one at a time. So pick one and make it the point of your focus for as long as it takes for you to feel safe, secure, and content with the skills you have acquired.

Remember, the prince did not start as a squire like the knight did. He was born into his title; his whole life has been a series of tasks, lessons, and events all leading him to the throne his father currently sits on, which means he has had some time to get to know all the elements of his earthy realm. But how well do you know yours? Let's say for argument's sake you have decided that you would like to use the Prince of Pentacles to represent your health. You want to feel safe and secure in the knowledge that you are doing the best for your body. So you go ahead and step into the prince's shoes.

The first thing you will notice is how the prince actually takes care of his body: how he grooms it, bathes it, and presents it. He will question you about how you do these things yourself. Then he will move on to food. You will notice his relationship to his food. He does not question if he will have enough, for in the prince's mind there is always plenty to nourish his body. Next he will move into exercise. Young princes move their bodies a lot. And seeing as this particular prince likes to be outdoors, you will be moved to do similar things. Go outdoors, explore the grass, dirt, trees, and sky.

Before you know it, you and the prince are feeling like one and the same energy. You feel more pride in your appearance, you stop questioning how your body is nourished because you trust yourself to always have an abundance of nutrient-rich fuel for your body, and you begin to naturally move more and spend more time outside. Now you are well on your way to mastering the one physical thing for which you have been training.

As a messenger

Knight—Just like the heavy earth they represent, the pentacles understand that time is actually on your side. Take a look at the natural world around you; its beauty was millions of years in the making. This knight understands that anything worthwhile—a happy home, a healthy body, a prosperous vocation—takes time. There truly is a slow yet focused energy connected to this card, which is more than likely why extroverts tend to receive this card frequently (well, the extroverts I read for do). If there was ever a card that said "it's not the destination, it's the journey" it would be the Knight of Pentacles.

If this card has shown up, you can be sure it is time to slow things down. You may have noticed the repetitive nature of this card already. That is because you need to repeat the same steps along your path each and every day in order to truly master them. Now is not the time for speed or haste, as these will only guarantee you lose ground, not gain it. Take the time to slow down now and you will move ahead in leaps and bounds farther down the path.

Prince—When the Prince of Pentacles rides into your world, you can be assured he is getting you ready for something bigger than your current circumstances. Thankfully, he is going to give you some time to get used to the idea because he knows you have a lot to learn. He also knows that you will start exactly where you are—not where you think you should be or where you feel more comfortable—in this moment of his appearance. If you don't start where you are, you will never be ready to start at all. This is something the prince knows only too well, because he must start where he is each and every day.

Slowly, surely, and deliberately he will move you along your path. He will make you stop from time to time so you can be fully aware of where you are in relation to where you came from. This prince sure is a smart one, which is probably just as well considering he will be king one day. Knowing how far you have traveled and how much farther you have to go is important. How will you ever be able to judge your progress if you never stop and take the time to reorient yourself?

With the Prince of Pentacles by your side, you can be sure you are on track to achieve your goal, dream, or wish. Rest assured in the knowledge that it will be done methodically, leaving no stone unturned along the road to success.

Knight of Wands: Explorer of Fire

It's important for the explorer to
be willing to be led astray.
ROGER VON OECH

Mutable Fire
Zodiac sign: Sagittarius
Keywords: Restless, risky, audacious

As a person

Knight—The Knight of Wands is a true adventurous knight. He is rightly named the Explorer of Fire in the Gaian Tarot because this knight really does get ants in his pants if he has to sit around for too long. To say that patience is not his strong suit would be an understatement. Standing still, waiting, and navel-gazing are not activities you will see this particular knight partaking in, not by choice anyway.

Restless, impulsive, and *movement-oriented* would be good adjectives for the energy of this card. It is not exactly a future-directed card, which is quite ironic because it is the future this knight is so eager to get to. Just take a look at the Knight of Wands in Llewellyn's Classic Tarot. His eyes are cast off in the distance and his horse is rearing up, impatient to burst forth with all the speed it can muster. Eager to get to where you are going, but wanting to be anywhere other than where you currently are.

Now don't get me wrong—there are times when the energy of this knight is needed, wanted, and welcomed. There are most definitely times when we truly need the Knight of Wands to light a fire under our ass and get us moving. There are also times when it is absolutely a good thing to be impulsive, spontaneous, and adventurous. Completely living in the moment. It's not the most desirable energy to be in all the time, frankly, unless of course you have an A-type personality and the whole point of your time here in this physical incarnation is to take risks and have extreme adventures.

The founders of Oxford University's Dangerous Sports Club were all true Knight of Wands personalities. Chris Baker, David Kirke, Ed Hulton, and Alan Weston were the first club to invent the modern-day bungee jump. They did their first jump on April 1, 1979. Like most Knight of Wands personalities, their vision spread like wildfire—pretty soon bungee clubs were forming all over the world. Such is the energy and rush of this fiery knight.

Prince—A real-life example of this energy is Prince Harry, the youngest son of Princess Diana and Prince Charles. There is a good chance Harry will never rule England. In fact, his chances of ever becoming a king are slim to none, especially considering his older brother William now has a successor, his own son, George.

Though he is much more level-headed and mellow now, Harry was a true Prince of Wands rapscallion. Harry has been making the headlines most of his life and for all the wrong reasons, especially during his formative years at boarding school. Although it is hard to say whether the loss of his mother and his genealogy being brought into question played a part in his wild ways, Harry was and can still be a prince on fire. He's ridden the wave of celebrity and royal bad boy for all it is worth; to his credit, he wasn't even trying that hard most of the time, typical of our Prince of Wands. Lighting fires without much effort is his specialty.

Just like all the princes and knights who came before him, Harry was sent off to military school to be trained in the ways of leadership and schooled in the art of discipline, after which a more skilled and diplomatic prince emerged, which is often the case. Although his innate nature is still the same, just as the Prince of Wands is, Harry learned to harness his energy and use it for more productive ventures. The Harry we see today would be a decent king, even if it is highly unlikely he would ever be allowed to so much as breathe on the throne. This is really the essence of this card, for regardless of whether you show up as the knight or the prince, you are in need of discipline, structure, and training. Your wand is your gift; the sparks are the seeds of your gift.

Now you need the focus, skill, and knowledge to make them flourish and grow.

As an archetypal influence

Knight—The Knight of Wands is the type of personality that would drop from a helicopter and snowboard down a very steep mountain while someone else records the whole thing on their GoPro. This person would like to bungee jump into volcanoes; base jumping is a relaxing way to spend a Sunday afternoon. The truth is, there are real-life Knights of Wands running around the globe right now, and as much as they seem to lead a dramatic and intensely interesting life, it's just not the type of life most of us could live or even want to for that matter. More to the point, we should not think we need to live a life like the Knights of Wands. But a little "daring greatly" energy never hurt anyone. And this is where the Knight of Wands and all his fiery energy come in handy.

This knight is all about pushing boundaries, setting new limits, and taking on the word "impossible" like it's a breakfast sandwich. These are all things we have to be willing to do if we want to manifest something different, bigger, or better into our lives. These are things we need to do if we want to heal or move on from the past. In other words, we all need to become the Knight of Wands at some point: eager to walk with the fire and blaze a path toward a happier, healthier, more abundant future.

The Explorer of Fire in the Gaian Tarot gives us a brilliant image of this archetype. This fire walker shows no fear as she walks through the burning loops and swirls of the flames around her. She even has a mask on, literally playing a part. This is what archetypal energy really is, a mask. It's a suit we put on when we need to be or do something that is not normal or comfortable to our natural state of being. On the other hand, our natural state of being changes and evolves over time. Who knows what will seem natural once we've finished our walk through fire?

Prince—Unlike the Knight of Wands, who in many respects has much more freedom when it comes to travel and passionate endeavors, the prince is in training to be king, or at least training to be a possible king. Due to his traveling ways and restless nature, it would not be unreasonable to think that this prince may be more of a diplomat in training, traveling to villages and other kingdoms on his father's behalf to broker deals, repair diplomatic ties, and strengthen bonds with allies. His charismatic nature and vibrant energy would make him perfect for such things…as long as he remembers to keep his temper in check. When a prince is reversed, you pretty much guarantee he has been unable to control his emotions and impulses. Getting him back in the upright position will benefit all involved.

It is important to remember that when dealing with any wands cards, we are dealing with reactionary energy. It is who they are by design, as they are meant to create sparks, start fires, and burn with passion. And sometimes they also cause explosions and destruction (but not all the time). As a diplomat, this prince would need to learn when to push the boundaries and when to hold back and maintain the spark of possibility. Political negotiations are tricky things, and it takes real skill to know when to make things move and when to let things simmer a while longer.

How good are you at negotiations? Do you know when to push for more? Can you keep a calm, rational head while allowing things to be discussed? Or are you attached to being right and having everything done your way?

These are all questions the Prince of Wands needs to ask himself again and again. He needs to keep his mind, actions, and emotions in check. This prince has great power but knowing when to unleash it and when to contain it may take him some time to learn. Which is why when this card shows up in a reading you may need to start documenting the way you deal with situations and people. Keep a record of what works and what has blown up in your face. Use this documentation as a way of honing your skills and fine-tuning your power. Soon you will be a lot more confident when it comes to asking for things, negotiating deals and agreements, and knowing when to move and move quickly without doubt and fear. All good positive attributes to have as a future king.

As a spiritual influence

Knight—This knight may very well love action but he is also very comfortable with the feelings and emotions his impulsive lifestyle create; you however may not be. Which is why working with the Knight of Wands is a fabulous idea if you are truly committed to bringing about big bodacious change in your life. For this knight can show you how to lean in and enjoy the thrill, while teaching you how not to be overly attached to the outcome. Remember, this knight moves on fast and there is no time for pity parties or guilt trips when you tag along with this particular member of the royal court.

So what changes do you want to make that scare the crap out of you?

For a lot of people, leaving things of comfort and security behind terrifies them. Like leaving a job they absolutely hate. Ending relationships that are soul sucking, or moving away from family and friends even though they feel like they are suffocating where they currently are. All three of these scenarios carry with them a heavy burden of attachment. Attachment causes suffering. Suffering is not something the Knight of Wands has time for. He or she has already moved on before the suffering energy can even show up.

This is where the Knight of Wands can be a real ally in your spiritual practice. He can guide you through the process of detachment. Burning away any cords that bind you is one of his greatest gifts. I mean, if ever there were a professional escape artist, it would be the Knight of Wands. His lack of fear is also a true gift here, for getting something wrong and failing don't bother him. If things don't go according to plan, he merely makes adjustments from where he now finds himself. This is an important attribute of this particular knight. He is not a planner, he is a doer, which means he only has mental space for one action step at a time. Once that step is completed, he then moves on to whatever presents itself next. Which is why there is no room for fear.

Fear tends to only be a problem for forward- or future-oriented thinkers…not the Knight of Wands. He is all about the now and only the now. So as you begin your process of detachment, the knight reminds you that tomorrow is of no consequence, only this moment right here and now. Deal with this moment and move into what is left in the following moment. I understand that may seem foolish to some people, but in actuality that is how this whole game of life thing works anyway. You can plan all you want, but life always has other plans for us and we very rarely see them coming. The Knight of Wands gets this, which is why he just lives every day like it's the day that everything could go right—or wrong. Either way, he makes it through.

So what attachments do you need to start cutting? Where can you use the Knight of Wands's assistance? How will you deal with the fear when it shows up for dinner?

Give yourself time to meditate on these points. Allow yourself some time to really identify where you are holding on to suffering. Just don't hesitate when this knight says "move"—he knows when to launch into action.

Prince—Knowing when to start a destructive fire and when to set off a spark of curiosity is something the prince must learn if he is to become a good leader and ruler. Therefore, a larger part of his training is going to be learning how to master, control, and honor the power in his wand, something that can be viewed both spiritually and sexually. In one sense, the prince is a walking royal gene pool. The blood that flows through his veins is important—so much so that like the princess, the prince can be forgotten about as an actual person and seem more like a tool to spread royal seed. Spilling the royal seed is another matter entirely, something you can only really get away with once you have become king. Princes, by contrast, can make a right royal mess by planting a seed in the wrong garden. What's a young, strong, handsome, and horny prince to do?

The royal seed can be used as a metaphor for a creative seed, or any other seed really! Also possible: the seed of an idea, the seed of healing, the seed of love. You decide what that seed is to you if and when this card presents itself in a reading or daily draw. We really do have to be careful where we plant our seeds. Creative seeds need special care and attention for them to grow. And as our dashing young prince knows only too well, distraction and temptation are everywhere.

No matter where you travel or whose company you find yourself in, the allure of temptation will be there. Learning how not to give in to this trap of desire is the spiritual part of this prince's journey. With a big wand comes great responsibility. And although there is really no need for judgment around this card, one will have to learn how to use that big wand for good, and not bad. Perhaps it would be more accurate to say that it's important to learn how to use that big wand for giving life, and not taking it away.

So what seeds are you walking around with inside of you? What do you need to do to make sure they are planted correctly? How will you use the wand of the knight to create what you require?

Fire can and does kill. It also restores and gives new life. It is a most powerful element, and the prince has many more lessons to learn. The important thing is to remember that mistakes can and will happen at this stage. It is a natural part of development. Bonds of trust may become lost, broken, or misguided; it is very easy to trust the wrong person when we have yet to learn the lesson of deceit. As a figurehead of his kingdom, this prince will have his fair share of rude awakenings and rites of passage. He will also be given many opportunities to show his skill and strengths, just as you will when this dashing prince blazes his way into your life.

As a messenger

Knight—The Knight of Wands in the Tarot of the Hidden Realm stands at the ready. He wants to teach you to tap into the rawness this element brings. He wants to show you the rush, the unknown, the liberation. He wants to teach you that it's all just part of the game and none of that should be taken so seriously. (Well, not yet, anyway.) The Knight of Wands reminds us that it is okay to explore, to see where creative energy takes us and not worry about what comes next. He says, "Just do this step. Now do this one, and now this one." As I said, it's really all good as long as you understand it's all temporary.

"Temporary" is the key word here, because before you even know what has happened, it will all be over. Just look at how the knight from the Tarot of the Hidden Realm crouches down among the brush, ready to spring at a moment's notice. His eyes are fixated on something just inside his field of vision. Like a cat he is pumped and tense, ready to take off when the moment of opportunity presents itself.

Can you say the same thing about the opportunities in your life? Are you ready to pounce on them the moment the timing is right? Or are you just sitting back, waiting to see what happens?

Learning to get out of your comfort zone and stretch your limits is a good thing. Learning to take on big change, big projects, or even big goals one step at a time is the key to success. Learning that failure isn't the end of the world is absolutely priceless.

Prince—There is no doubt of the rarefied space this prince now occupies. But it does serve him, just as it will serve you when this card comes galloping into your life. You will find yourself full of life, energy, and curiosity. You will feel reckless, inspired, spontaneous, and like somewhat of a rebel; temptations will be around every corner. But it also means things are getting very interesting for you indeed, as your journey is heating up; at this point it's all or nothing, baby!

This prince isn't a quitter, that's for sure. He's getting results one way or another. And so too shall you if you can manage to stand in his energy long enough. Just don't expect this prince to stick around once he has what he came for—he is not interested in long-term commitments. You can tell by his incredibly short attention span. In many respects, the Prince of Wands is all about the chase. After he has what he wants, he will release the energy and walk away, on to the next conquest and out of your life.

Your creative gifts are part of who you are. You can't escape them, even if you try. Best to learn to deal with them, learn, and master them before you become destructive. If we do not draw the creative life fire out of us and birth it into the world, what happens to it? Does it die or does it instead burn through us until it causes us to be drained of life? Let's hope the energy of this card keeps you moving enough so you never have to find out.

Knight of Cups: Explorer of Water

*Some say that the age of chivalry is past, that the spirit
of romance is dead. The age of chivalry is never past,
so long as there is a wrong left unredressed on earth.*
CHARLES KINGSLEY

Mutable Water
Zodiac sign: Pisces
Keywords: Romantic, fickle, gallant

As a person

Knight—Of all the knights, the Knight of Cups is more in
love with the idea of being a knight than actually having to
partake in the roles and responsibilities connected to his title.
The Knight of Cups loves the romance and art associated with

his station: dressing up, pageantry, ritual, and spectacle. He is the poet, dreamer, and feeler of all the knights. Wherever this knight goes, romance is sure to follow. And with romance comes those who just want to be in his presence. Although many cannot see his vision or even believe completely in his romantic version of life, they do often get swept up in the feeling of his convictions. There is no doubt this knight spends a little too much time with stars in his eyes, but you cannot help being moved by the depths of his beliefs. People are often drawn to the person who seems to have no doubt in their beliefs and convictions, but this is not always a good thing.

Because of his super-sensitive nature, the Knight of Cups can also be a target for nonvirtuous people. He can find himself being bullied and made into a target by all those who feel threatened by his vision of how the world could be. This can either end in the start of a movement toward social change or it can end in violence. For me personally, one of the most famous Knight of Cups we've had in our modern world is John Lennon. John's vision is still held on to today by those who celebrate the day of his death each and every year. That said, holding the vision is only the first step. At some point the Knight of Cups will have to stop dreaming and start doing, or the world he dreams of will only ever live inside his head.

Prince—To say this prince is a ladies' man would be an understatement. Women seem to flock to two types of men: the physically stunning jock and the romantically sensitive brooder. The Prince of Cups has the art of brooding down to a science. Pouty, fickle, and moody, this young prince has much to learn when it comes to pulling his head out of his own dream cloud. This broodiness is captured in the card from the Tarot of the Hidden Realm. I mean, this guy looks like the weight of the world is squarely on his shoulders. Some would argue that he is just so sensitive, he has no other choice but to get lost in his own being. The truth is that he can master his gifts, which are in the cup itself, and be of real service to his kingdom and people.

Finding ways to channel this constantly flowing energy is the prince's main life lesson. He needs to find outlets for all the information he receives and all the feelings that flood his soul. This is why many people with Prince of Cups personalities end up as writers, composers, musicians, artists, dancers, and actors. These creative outlets allow the prince to indulge his emotional ways productively. Unlike the other princes, this one can seem to take a little more time to mature and grow into his kingly skin, but he will eventually get there. Just look at Elton John, who by the way is a perfect Prince of Cups character. It took him decades and a team of support people to get him where he is today. But his passion, vision, and sheer creative brilliance won out in the long run. So it is with the Prince of Cups.

As an archetypal influence

Knight—In Llewellyn's Classic Tarot, the Knight of Cups has his eyes closed. Even though his horse appears to be in motion, it is almost as if he wants to "feel" his journey, not see it. He wants to connect with the energy of his ride rather than control it. He looks like he is more in a state of walking prayer, or more to the point, riding prayer. He trusts the horse underneath him to support him, guide him, and keep him safe. Such is how it goes for this knight's intuitive power. He finds it much easier to connect to the "vibes" around him than the people who want to be by his side.

Contemplation, meditation, and melancholy are part of the archetypal energy of this card, helping us understand the Knight of Cups's romantic nature a little better. For clarity, what I mean by "romance" is not about courtship, dating, or swooning over the idea of romantic love. The romance this knight seeks is life itself. His great love affair is his life as a knight. So his love is for finding the depth and beauty of what is in him and around him.

In many respects, the Knight of Cups tends to see love through rose-colored glasses. He is a lover, not a fighter, and would be more inclined to ride for peace and love than war. Because this knight sees the beauty in life, he also tends to want to spread it around to others. This can often lead the knight into melancholy and heartbreak, as very few people view the world through the same lens as him. Where he sees possibilities, others see struggle. Where he sees redemption, others see suffering. No matter where he travels, he finds it almost impossible to find others who align to his views of the world. This often leads our dreamy knight into isolation, yet being alone is torture for this very social archetype.

Prince—The Prince of Cups who sees no real future and does not believe he should be in service to others is his own worst enemy. Left with no direction, this prince can become withdrawn, can become disconnected, and can easily turn to distraction. One could say this is the card in its reverse position, but that is not always the case—he could still be in his own power and control of his own path even if it is a destructive one.

Reversals tend to signify a block, kink, or disruption to the flow of energy from the suit, but honestly the Prince of Cups is far too clever to be unaware of what he is doing. He can be in total control and fully flowing as both his light and dark selves. This is the trouble with water—it flows wherever it is directed; good or bad have nothing to do with it. For the sake of argument, let us presume, as we have with the other princes, that the Prince of Cups is going to be king. He will see a crown placed on his head and will be handed the controlling power of his father's kingdom. He needs to know how to keep himself emotionally balanced and learn how to feel and not be overwhelmed. As well, he needs to be able to lead with a cool head and a compassionate heart.

This prince will also need a lot of help. He will need a mentor, teacher, or guide to instruct him. You see, water is a tricky thing, as it flows through everything. It thus feels everything and is connected to all life. Learning what is yours, what is someone else's, and what needs your attention isn't the easiest skill to learn. It takes time, patience, and discipline. It requires a clear head and an open heart. No matter how badly the Prince of Cups wants to drown his feelings or succumb to melancholy, he cannot. Instead, he needs to be like water and feel everything, yet hold on to none of it.

The responsibility to his kingdom demands nothing less, and this is truly what separates the energy of the knight and prince. Sure, the prince can pretend for a while that he is a playboy and can woo princesses and write beautiful poetry. He can even overindulge his senses and desires, but it is all temporary. The pretending will and must come to an end. He must stand up and be responsible for himself and his people. This is important when the Prince of Cups shows up in readings because whatever is going on right now will require you to put away your childish ways and take a stand for yourself and those you love.

As a spiritual influence

Knight—When the Knight of Cups comes up in a reading for myself or my clients, the very first thing I think about is the possibility of a quest. This knight always reminds me of one of the knights from the Round Table, on a quest to find the Holy Grail, which would be the chalice or cup he rides with in his hands. Quests are not something many people think of doing these days, but they are making a comeback in some of the most interesting and profound ways.

In *The Happiness of Pursuit: Finding the Quest That Will Bring Purpose to Your Life*, author, entrepreneur, and quest master Chris Guillebeau documents not only his own huge quest to travel to every country on the planet, but also the real-life quests of everyday people like you and me. Some of the stories will bring you to tears, while others will restore your faith in humanity. Some of the quests documented in the book are large and bold, and others are small and practical. All of them were deeply personal to the person undertaking the quest.

So what is a quest and how does one walk in the footsteps of the Knight of Cups and take one?

It is very easy, actually. You find something you wish to do, i.e., the quest. Give yourself a firm starting point and a very clear finishing point, and off you go. It could be knitting a hundred hats for cancer patients in a year. It could be attending one conference a month for five years. It could be as bold as Chris's own quest, which took him ten years to complete. The size and time it will take are irrelevant. What is important is that it starts and then ends. A quest is not ongoing. I repeat—a quest is not ongoing. It could, however, spark a lifelong habit.

The Knight of Cups needs to be of service. It is what he was born to do. He needs something to put all of his emotional and intuitive energy into and there is nothing more perfect than a quest. So if this starry-eyed knight makes his way into your reading or daily draw, ask yourself what quest is waiting for you to undertake it. When will you begin?

Prince—We all need romance and feeling in our lives, as none of us can really enjoy life without opening our hearts to feeling. But we cannot lose ourselves to our emotions or our dreams. Instead, we must learn to create, give birth, and be of service. Just like the prince, you don't have to do this alone. In fact, you *can't* do it alone; you will need assistance, be it a teacher, mentor, or coach. Someone outside yourself must help you direct your flow. They must show you how to use your power and keep you focused and aware.

Do you have a spiritual teacher or mentor right now? If not, now would be the perfect time to get one. The Prince of Cups has some very special gifts, but they need the guiding hand of someone older and wiser than he is. Seeking out a spiritual teacher is the first step in understanding that you really do have a place and purpose in this big, hectic world. Finding the right teacher may take some time. In my Buddhist practice, students spend a lot of time—and I mean a *lot* of time—talking about how to choose a spiritual teacher. We are asked to explore what it means to be a spiritual student and how to know when we should stay and when we should lock up the wallet and run for the hills. The main lesson is that we must be discerning.

If the Prince of Cups has shown up in your reading or daily draw, start journaling about what sort of spiritual studies you would like to undertake. Then make a list of at least twenty possible teachers. Do not limit yourself here, as it really will take time to find the right teacher for your specific journey. Seek out these teachers and study them. Watch how they live their lives. Make sure they practice what they preach and are constantly partaking in virtuous acts. Beware the egocentric guru who claims he has already reached enlightenment, for if he is still walking around in our physical world, he has not yet reached it.

As a messenger

Knight—Like all knights, the Knight of Cups must learn how to deal with his gift; these lessons are summed up brilliantly in the Explorer of Water card from the Gaian Tarot. This Knight of Cups rides a surfboard and learns how to navigate the unpredictable ocean swells. Waves are temperamental things and can change their mood without warning. One minute you will be enjoying the ride of your life, and the next thing you know, you have been dumped on the rocks.

The suit of cups is like riding a temperamental ocean wave, and if this knight is to ever master his craft, he is going to have to get used to crashing. So it goes with emotions. One minute they are up and we are happy and adrenaline is pumping, and the next they are down and we feel ourselves being pulled under the swell to the point of drowning. This never-ending journey between extremes is the Knight of Cups's journey. He very rarely finds middle ground, yet it is the middle ground he truly needs to seek.

When this knight rides his way into your life, grab your wetsuit because one thing is for sure—the ride is going to be anything but calm.

Prince—The Prince of Cups doesn't have the luxury of a lifetime to learn how to ride the waves of his emotional, creative, intuitive sense of self. If he is to become king, he needs to master his element sooner rather than later. The prince's responsibilities are far more pressing than those of our knight. Because of the knight's station, he can be as indulgent as he wishes with his watery ways. The prince, however, cannot. Well, maybe he could, but I don't like his chances of survival if he insists on clinging to his adolescent ways, especially if his next step is to be king.

A weak leader is unable to make hard decisions. A leader who is lost to the world of dreams and fantasies never gets to see his vision fulfilled. And a leader who spends all of his time dulling his senses will eventually lose his crown and all his power. The road may be hard for this prince, but eventually he will get it together. And when he does, he will be as powerful as a tsunami with the compassionate heart of a monk.

Knight of Swords: Explorer of Air

Do not dwell in the past, do not dream of the future,
concentrate the mind on the present moment.

Buddha

Mutable Air
Zodiac sign: Gemini
Keywords: Fearless, lofty, philosophical

As a person

Knight—If ever there were a knight to represent the knights of old, it would be the Knight of Swords. Riding full speed on his trusty steed, sword raised and forward in full armor, Llewellyn's Classic Tarot shows a knight who is the embodiment of a feudal knight. With his fully polished armor, majestic horse, and battle-ready appearance, this knight is the knight of all knights. He will be able to recite the contents of the knight's code word for word and will more than likely teach it to someone else later on.

Statesman, political adviser, and all-round good guy, the Knight of Swords is all about morals and correct conduct. His word is his bond and he would rather die with honor than bring shame to himself or his king. The Knight of Swords holds himself to a higher standard than most, for he prides himself on being just and true. In practice, it means really having a good grasp on that sword of his, as discipline is a way of life to the Knight of Swords. He is almost zenlike in his daily life; he doesn't just go through the day mindlessly performing duties and tasks, he does them in a state of mindful meditation.

The quest for the higher realms of the mind is important to this knight. He has a thirst for knowledge and believes wisdom is the key to true inner power. It is a shame that this sort of knight is not as abundant as it once was. Every so often, however, you will see people who understand the importance of education. Martin Luther King Jr. and Maya Angelou were real Knight of Swords personalities. Their weapon of choice was their mind, and they encouraged others to educate themselves and find true freedom. They understood that to commit to a fight worthy of their gifts, it had to benefit as many people as possible and not just themselves. This sort of selflessness is just another day at the office for the Knight of Swords.

Prince—The Prince of Swords is in many ways the student of higher learning. Regardless of whether he is a college or university student or a solo student of life, he is on a quest to know as much as he can. His thirst for knowledge is insatiable, like a junkie always looking for his next fix. This need to know more is fueled by the sword he carries at his side. With each swing of his blade he makes room for more and more knowledge.

The Prince of Swords is not quite at the stage where he has refined his knowledge to where it will be of benefit to his role as king—but he will get there eventually. For now it's like someone has handed him the secret book to the universe and he just wants to soak it all up.

Have you ever had a feeling of wanting to know more about something? Have you ever had your curiosity piqued so much that you can't think of anything else until you have found some sort of reconciliation with whatever it is you seek?

We have all had times when our minds have become obsessed with thoughts and ideas. The difference between the king and the prince is that one knows which of these ideas is worth pursuing and which are merely distractions. This can be a big problem for the young prince. He can get very, very distracted, which is why every so often that sword comes in handy. It can cut the ties that bind him to distracting thoughts, allowing him to once again free himself only to repeat the cycle of his journey.

As an archetypal influence

Knight—When the Knight of Swords comes up in a reading, it is important to ask a few questions, as this knight often holds more questions then he does answers. Let's take a closer look at the knight from Llewellyn's Classic Tarot.

What exactly is this knight charging off to? Is it battle? Is he just practicing? Is he playing? What is going on beyond the frame of the card itself?

The Knight of Swords looks like he is protecting something, but what could it be? Could it in fact be the mind? The suit of swords can really be a mental suit, and by that I mean, it has the ability to drive you nuts, batty, and out of your mind, as the mind is capable of creating pretty much anything. Our knight may very well be charging to fight off an imagined fear or a made-up enemy.

The Hierophant   Knight of Swords   8 of Cups   3 of Swords

Knight of Swords reading: What is he defending or fighting?
(Llewellyn's Classic Tarot)

In order for you to see what the knight is attacking and what he is defending, you will need to pay attention to the card or cards surrounding him in a spread or reading. This also means paying attention to the direction the knight is facing. In Llewellyn's Classic Tarot, the Knight of Swords is charging to the left of the card, possibly implying he is defending his future from the demons of his past. Meaning any card to the left of this knight will identify this past issue, belief, or situation. The cards to his right will give you an indication of what he is defending, in both his current reality and his immediate future. It will be up to you to decide if the knight in your reading is defending the right thing or if he's just wasting precious mental energy on an imagined threat.

In contrast, the Knight of Swords in the Tarot of the Hidden Realm looks upward and to the right. This knight stands in a very defensive pose, yet he seems to not really understand that which he is defending himself from. Perhaps this is because he is walking into the unknown. He faces the future like a true warrior. He feels totally prepared and ready to take on whatever happens to come his way. He seems like such a brave and noble knight. But the truth is he is only as brave as his mind allows him to be, which is an important aspect of this archetype. You are only that which your mind allows you to be. Or in this case, the knight is only what his mind allows him to be.

Prince—Princes in many ways tend to straddle past and future. They walk into an already established kingdom that has been ruled and governed by the laws of the last king. If all is well, some of these laws will remain in place. But most princes dream of putting their own mark on the world, spending time thinking about how they would either make existing systems better or get rid of outdated ways to bring forth a new age. The direction your prince faces will be important.

The Explorer of Air in the Gaian Tarot looks straight ahead. He is not allowing the past or the future to control his sight. Instead, he is focused on the moment he now finds himself in. High up in the trees above the noise of the day-to-day, time has no real meaning. Here he can lean into the moment that presents itself. Here with the birds he offers a third option, a third and more desired way of being, the now. Sometimes neither the past or the future are relevant in the decisions of the present. Sometimes you just have to see what is actually there and decide accordingly. This is a gift the Prince of Swords is learning to master.

Mastering the here and now is one of the hardest gifts to deal with. Far too often the mind is fixated on what is missing, not what is there. How many times have you found yourself judging your present set of circumstances by what you feel is missing? Maybe it's the money you don't have or the people who didn't show up or the result was not at all what you expected. All of these are distractions. They take your mind away from the present moment and place it in either the past or the fantasized future.

If you were preparing to take the throne, where do you think your mind should be? Should it be on the ghost of the past or the fear of the unknown future? Would it be best to focus, center, and stay in the right here and now?

It takes tremendous discipline to keep your mind on the moment and soak up every drop of what is and not be swayed by what was or what could be. We could say that walking this path is like walking in meditation, and perhaps that is exactly what this young prince is here to show us.

As a spiritual influence
Knight—The Knight of Swords reminds us that we have the ability to take on whatever we choose, as long as we believe we can. This card is about those moments when the mind is

as focused and disciplined as our desire. As the Buddha once said, "What you believe, you achieve."

So what do you believe about your own personal strength? What do you believe is true about the stories you tell about yourself? And what do you believe is worth fighting for?

The sword itself may be key to answering some of these questions and clearing up any confusion. You see, the sword the knight wields can be used to cut the cords of the past, to cut the hooks of fear and doubt, and to clear the pathway of the less traveled road. The sword is a powerful tool and it doesn't have to be real. Your mind can do everything the sword can; all you have to do is make the decision.

Decide the past is done with, decide to stop living your life by the terms spelled out by doubt and fear, decide that you want to do things you haven't done before. Everything the sword can do happens in your mind, and it all starts with the decision. A decision is a commitment, the commitment you have made with yourself and the divine. It is an energetic bond that shows the price you will pay for the result you say you wish to have.

But understand that no decision is good and no decision is bad. It is just a decision. Because this is where the Knight of Swords can get a little mental if you allow it. Let's say you make a decision, you follow through with your commitment, and it doesn't work out at all the way you had hoped or dreamed it would. In fact, it ended up being quite a nightmare. So you begin to doubt your ability to make the right decision. This makes your inner knight start to create imagined threats and make-believe battles, in turn creating all sorts of uncertainty in your daily life.

You start to use your sword not for moving forward but for self punishment. You cut yourself with the berating comments, hateful thoughts, and untrue stories about who you are and what you are capable of. You turn your back on your future and begin to battle with your past, and because you have trained your mind to believe whatever story you tell it, it acts accordingly. Remember that all knights are in training—they never stop, which means whatever skills you give your knight to train with, he is going to work to master them. This is why it is so important to train your Knight of Swords to empower you, strengthen you, and keep moving you forward. Otherwise you give the knight permission to slowly bleed you to death with every cut of his sword.

Prince—The Explorer of Air in the Gaian Tarot seems to show us how to balance all of this mental energy. Get to higher ground and change your perspective, or as Dr. Wayne Dyer used to say, "Change the way you look at things, and the things you look at change." Sometimes we can allow our minds to be focused on such a small part of a problem, solution, or situation. This narrowness disallows further information to enter. But by removing or distancing ourselves and shifting our gaze, we can see things in a whole new way. We are like the young Explorer of Air, climbing high into the trees to broaden our view—sometimes we have to move.

What point of view do you currently hold? Are you too close or too far away? Would you say from your current viewpoint you can see all possibilities or only a few?

The prince offers you another way to feed your hunger for knowledge and maintain a more balanced approach to life.

His advice is pretty simple: change your point of perspective. This not only allows the mind to shift gears and refocus on collecting new data, but it also allows the swords to cut away anything that could be blocking your vision.

As a messenger
Knight—When the Knight of Swords comes bounding into your reading or daily draw, there is no doubt he is going to call you out on your personal, professional, and spiritual conduct. He is going to make you question your thoughts, beliefs, and values. Not to mention he opens the door to higher realms of knowledge and understanding. This may indicate it is time to pursue more education or seek out a mentor or coach, someone who can take you from where you are to where you want to be. This knight is an intellectual by nature and prefers his learning in book form. If this seems out of alignment with your current learning style, it will be up to you to find a teacher who can give you the lessons you need in a way that expands your mind without causing confusion and distraction.

Like all the other knights, the Knight of Swords means movement. You can either go quietly or go kicking and screaming—it's your choice. But either way, you will be moving on to something new, even if it is subtle and small. For that reason, it is always a good idea to be very aware when the Knight of Swords is around, as he will expect you to mentally keep up with him. He might just bring his sword down on you hard if you fail to follow his quest. It bears repeating: you *will* be moving, but how your journey plays out is entirely up to you.

Prince—When the Prince of Swords shows up in a reading, he is extending an invitation to come practice walking with him. He wants to be your study partner as you yourself learn how to stay focused and centered. He will even graciously let you use his sword so you can cut the hooks of the past and the threads of desire you have wrapped around your future.

No matter how you swing this particular sword, something is going to get cut. Beliefs, fears, dreams, ideas, and decisions—nothing is safe from this prince's sword. The sword can liberate or hurt; it's entirely up to you. The power is in your mind as this is your sword and your mind can be used to empower you or destroy you. Your mind can become confused, scared, and scattered or it can be controlled, focused and aware. Whether you choose to ride into battle, walk the path of the unknown, or head for higher ground, at some point you have to engage the logic and reason of your sword.

Connecting Exercises and Spreads
Chivalry and the knightly code
When one hears the word "chivalry," images of knights on white horses riding in to save fair maidens tend to come to mind. Yet this simplistic romantic notion of chivalry is a bit off the mark in relation to what it meant to the knights of the medieval period. Chivalry was a much more complex ideology with many moving parts; rescuing fair maidens was never actually mentioned. In the book *Rules for a Knight*, author Ethan Hawke introduces us to the code of conduct that forms this ideology. This list was handed down by one of his ancestors, who was an actual knight in the British royal court.

The twenty rules are as follows:

- Solitude

- Humility

- Gratitude

- Pride

- Cooperation

- Friendship

- Forgiveness

- Honesty

- Courage

- Grace

- Patience

- Justice

- Generosity

- Discipline

- Dedication

- Speech

- Faith

- Equality

- Love

- Death

As you can see, this is a pretty extensive list of rules and attributes that all knights were meant to uphold and practice on a regular basis. When I first read this list, my first thought was, why was this not taught to everyone? If we all lived by this sort of code of conduct, imagine how much nicer the world might be. I have started working with this list in my daily life and I have to say, focusing on things like dedication, grace, or even pride deliberately as a spiritual practice sure makes you realize just how much of your life is lived on autopilot. Which is why I thought it would make a wonderful exercise for this chapter.

Look at the list and pick one attribute to focus on for the day. You could do this for a week or even a month, if you wanted. For now, observe how making one of these your deliberate point of focus changes your day.

Let's say you pick humility. How would you humbly go about your day? What does humility actually mean to you? What thoughts, actions, and feelings are aligned with humility?

What about speech? How would you make your words count during the day? In what way would you make sure that your words were received clearly? What would you need to do to make sure your words were not seen as weapons?

Or let's say you choose to focus on pride. Where does pride stop being ego-based and start being spirit-based? How do you show pride in yourself and those around you? What does pride even mean to you?

As you can see, this is not such an easy task. I figure if this list of rules was good enough for the knights to live by for five hundred years, it is certainly good enough for us to explore in modern-day experience. If you want to take this exercise a step further, pick a card to work with alongside the word or rule you select. Perhaps with courage you would pick Strength, the 3 of Swords, or even the 10 of Swords. You can even select the card randomly and see what you need to focus on in relation to the rule you have picked.

Play with this exercise and record it in your journal or tarot diary. If nothing else, it will expand your awareness and make you more focused and strategic in your thoughts, feelings, and actions—much like a knight.

How Far Can I Go? Spread

How often have you heard yourself ask, "How much longer is this going to take?" Like most people, probably very often. But this is not a question that bothers a knight as they are on their journey for life. Instead the knight asks, "How far can I go?" Do you notice the difference in these two questions? One is limited, the other is expansive. When we are only concerned with limit, be it time, energy, or resources, we miss an opportunity to truly accomplish something with depth, skill, and passion. Lucky for all of us, the knights of the tarot court are here to remind us that life is an endless journey of expansion.

This spread is designed to push you past your current set of limitations and show you what else is possible when you are not looking for a finish line. This is a good spread to do when you feel stuck or frustrated.

First, remove the knights from your deck. It's perfectly fine if you have princes instead of knights, as either will work nicely for this spread. Place them face up, one under the other in a straight line in this order:

- *Knight* or *Prince of Swords*: Your mind

- *Knight* or *Prince of Wands*: Your actions

- *Knight* or *Prince of Cups*: Your feelings

- *Knight* or *Prince of Pentacles*: Your resources

Now pick up your remaining cards and shuffle. Place three cards in a row next to each knight. Total, you should have sixteen cards in front of you. Refer to this diagram.

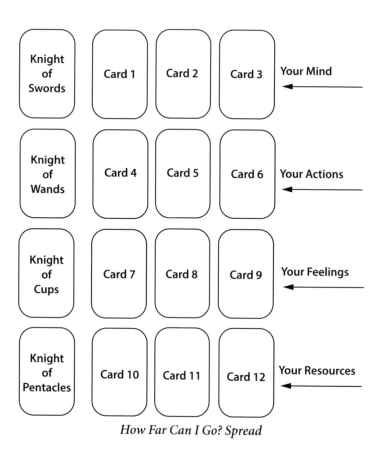

How Far Can I Go? Spread

- *Column one* alerts you to where things stand now

- *Column two* lets you know where they need to be to move you forward

- *Column three* shows what needs to happen to move you from where you are to where you need to be.

Following is a sample spread (on next page):

Row 1, The Mind—7 of Pentacles, Ace of Cups, and Fortune Faery. In this row I can see just how limited the present mind is. The 7 of Pentacles is actually a card about waiting. Yet next to the Ace of Cups, we can see that waiting and doing nothing is not at all what we should be doing to move us forward. Waiting implies the question "How much longer?" whereas the Ace of Cups says, "It's here to enjoy now!" The Ace of Cups wants us to overflow with joy and get swept along with the unlimited energy of the life-giving water. Quite the contrast of the waiting around energy of the 7 of Pentacles. But how do we do this? With the Fortune Faery. Start counting your blessings. There is a game you can play that keeps the mind engaged in gratitude: simply make a point of mentally blessing everything you come in contact with during the day. This in and of itself is an active exercise that allows us to shift our awareness from waiting to cocreating.

Knight of Swords 7 of Pentacles Ace of Cups Fortune Faery

Knight of Wands 6 of Wands Shadowdance 8 of Pentacles

Knight of Cups 2 of Pentacles Queen of Swords Ace of Swords

Knight of Pentacles 3 of Swords 10 of Wands 7 of Wands

How Far Can I Go? (Sample Reading)
(Tarot of the Hidden Realm)

Row 2, Actions—6 of Wands, Shadowdance, and 8 of Pentacles. In this row we can see that the the current actions are already celebrating with the victory card of the 6 of wands as if there is nothing left to be done. Yet the Devil card (here, Shadowdance) lets us know that this is an illusion—and a dangerous one, at that. Instead, we should be fully present and aware of our current level of engagement with our actions. We are able to see the Devil's liberation aspect more than anything else. For the Devil shows us both sides of an outcome, one that can cause us more suffering and one that can release us from suffering. He doesn't care which one you pick; he merely shows you your options. So how do we stop our actions from causing us suffering? Through the 8 of Pentacles. This card shows us that our work is far from over; we have many more skills to refine and master, quite a ways from the victory dance in the 6 of Wands.

Row 3, Feelings—2 of Pentacles, Queen of Swords, and the Ace of Swords: Living in a feeling universe should make us extra mindful of our emotions, yet surprisingly it very rarely does. Here, the 2 of Pentacles symbolizes feeling bound by duty and responsibility. Like the 7 of Pentacles in the first row, this is a pretty limiting card that tends to imply a level of waiting for something to end. Yet the card next to it seems to imply this is not the case. The Queen of Swords knows only too well that in order to take control of your life, you need to sharpen your mind and get your thoughts and feelings in alignment with where you want to be. In other words, our feelings should not be concerned with the limit we feel we have and instead be free to explore the thrill of what is yet to come. To move into this level of anticipation, we have the Ace of Swords. The Ace of Swords wants to put us on alert to all opportunities, for when we feel stuck or bound in the 2 of Pentacles, we don't look around for opportunities. Instead we become fixated on the only two objects in our filed of vision. The Ace wants us to reconcile this gap between the 2 of Pentacles and the Queen of Swords by shifting our focus to the possibility of more.

Row 4, Resources—3 of Swords, 10 of Wands, and 7 of Wands: This row really wraps up the story as what we think, feel, and do creates the physical world around us. In other words, everything we see, feel, touch, hear, smell, and interact with is a creation of our thoughts, emotions, and responses to them. It is no wonder this row starts with the 3 of Swords, for if ever there were a card about suffering, this would be it. Let's face it, when you are stuck in a state of "how much longer," you are suffering. Interestingly, the card following it is the 10 of Wands. Traditionally this is also a card of burdens, but it can also be a card of liberation. And how we make our way to that liberation is in the 7 of Wands. There is no doubt that these are pretty heavy cards; none seem overly joyful. Yet, they are the result of the current set of vibrations coming from the heart, mind, and body. The 7 of Wands is a standing-up-for-yourself-type of card. When this card presents itself, you either have to put up or shut up, hence the liberation aspect of the 10 of Wands. You either have to pick up your wands and keep going, or have their weight burden you while you wallow in your own self-pity. Wallowing is not an option for a knight—he has to keep going, for failure is not part of his knightly code.

If you narrow this reading down to the last column, we can see that there is so much more to do and achieve. The Fortune Faery is still looking upon us with favor, and the 8 of Pentacles is more than ready and able to keep up with these expansive opportunities. The Ace of Swords is alert and aligned to all ideas, flashes of inspiration, and creative visions, while the 7 of Wands is ready to take on all that comes her way. In this column there is a lot of movement, anticipation, and energy, which is quite the contrast to the still, stagnant energy of the current situation seen in column one.

This spread will give you much to work with and work on. So take your time with it and explore each row, one at a time. You may find that this spread actually gives you months of information in it, another reason it is extremely helpful when you feel yourself grinding to a halt or hitting that proverbial brick wall. After working with this spread, you will also learn to catch yourself when you feel the need to ask, "How much longer?" and allow you to shift the energy into "How far can I go?"

four

The Queens

Because I am a woman, I must make unusual efforts to succeed. If I fail, no one will say, "She doesn't have what it takes." They will say, "Women don't have what it takes."

CLARE BOOTHE LUCE, AUTHOR,
POLITICIAN, AND US AMBASSADOR

....

Mother, *Maiden, Crone*—so many faces, so many titles and hats. Women of the tarot court have had to be all things to all people, all of the time. Their roles as queens, mothers, wives, peacekeepers, negotiators, and mentors are roles they must play twenty-four hours a day, seven days a week. There are no days off. These queens represent the successes and failures of all women. No matter how she shows up in the cards, these rules still apply as much today as they did when the queens first took their place on the faces of playing and gaming cards back in the fifteenth century.

History, Myth, and Legend

The title "queen" has changed and evolved over the course of royal history. Once, it only meant "wife of the king." The title was only something to distinguish the station of one court woman over the other. It brought with it no power, respect, or safety. It wasn't until the eleventh century that this title was challenged. Henry I's daughter Matilda was a real female king (not queen) in her own right. Her coronation was written into law, and for the first time in history, the title of queen meant more than a king's wife.

Unfortunately for Matilda, it was all fabulous in theory, but no one was able to follow through in practice. Matilda was never crowned, and those who once supported the idea of a female king with real power turned their backs the moment they were expected to back their ideology up with action. Matilda's grandson Richard, who became King Richard I, placed his mother Eleanor in power as regent while he went off to fight the third Crusade. As luck would have it, Eleanor's reign ended up being quite lengthy. Although not a female king in her own right by coronation, for all intents and purposes Eleanor was calling the shots and ruling the vast empire her late husband Henry II built. This made Eleanor one of the most powerful women in the high Middle Ages.

It took another five hundred years, however, to break the limitations the title of queen held over women in the Renaissance English court. In 1559, the Tudors and England had run out of options. Elizabeth I was crowned, and with her the keys to the kingdom opened a new set of doors. Our world of tarot, however, was created a hundred years before Elizabeth I shattered the first of many glass ceilings for queens everywhere. Initially, the court cards were very much based on the roles governed by the very real courts of the time.

But let's back it up just for a minute. In fact, let's back it up about two thousand years before our medieval queens. Let's take a peek at a woman of the ancient world who also held but shared the title of female king, Hatshepsut. In many respects, the female revolution began in 1478 BCE, for it was in this year that Hatshepsut took the throne in her own right. Hatshepsat ruled for more than twenty years, opening up new trade routes and expanding her kingdom. Yet despite all of her hard work and dedication to her people, her reign was wiped from the slate of history like it never even happened, buried deep between the cracks of all the men who came before and after her.

The four queens of the tarot carry with them the weight of all women who came before them. In each of these cards resides the stories, struggles, and victories of all the powerful women of history. As the roles of women have evolved, so too have the images of the tarot queens. In this respect, our tarot queens pay homage to women like Matilda, Eleanor, Elizabeth, and Hatshepsut, all the while showing women of the modern world what is possible when they step into and claim their power.

This chapter is dedicated to the great women of the tarot court. Please know that although this chapter does gender the queens as women, this in no way means that men cannot align to or harness the archetypal energy of these queens. If anything, the great ladies of the tarot court help us all to get in touch with the strong yin energy that pumps through us regardless of whatever gender we happen to identify with.

Each of the queens in this chapter belongs to their own kingdom and are guardians of their own personal element. It is their responsibility to make sure their court runs smoothly and that all the guests and visitors are safe and well taken care of. For those queens who are rulers in their own right, they will be far too busy running the kingdom to be worrying about guests and visitors.

Queens have many roles and responsibilities. Some merely continue bloodlines and never get a chance to rule anything. Others, however, are born into power and spend their lives putting their realm above all else. Mary, Queen of Scots, is an excellent example of this. Duty and obligation governed every part of her life and eventually drove her mad. That said, not everyone can survive the stress of ruling. Some queens end up ruling by divine destiny. Elizabeth I is a fine example. By rights, she should never have seen the throne, yet she stepped into the role of queen as if she had been groomed for it her whole life.

When a queen comes up in your reading, you may need to consider if this is an energy you were born to embrace or if you have to play the part out of necessity. Sometimes being a queen is a lifelong occupation, and other times it's a passing phase. You will need to consider whether or not you are ready and able to step into these roles and responsibilities the queen has to offer. Each grand dame brings with her a special power and divine gift, each intimately connected to the element she represents.

Queen of Pentacles: Guardian of Earth

If you look at what you have in life, you'll
always have more. If you look at what you
don't have in life, you'll never have enough.
Oprah Winfrey

Cardinal Earth
Zodiac sign: Capricorn
Keywords: Dependable, patient, enduring

As a person

If ever there was a queen to carry on a bloodline, it would be
the Queen of Pentacles. She is in many respects the queen of
fertility. Connected to the ever-giving bounty of the earth, the
Queen of Pentacles is a symbol of multiplying opportunities.

This is probably why she is often depicted with animal totems, such as the rabbit, often the totem of fertility and multiplicity. This queen is down-to-earth and very at home sitting in her garden or harvesting her bounty from the fields.

Although this queen can be seen as one who is more at home close to the earth, you may just be selling her short. The Queen of Pentacles tends to be the archetype of the modern female entrepreneur, a woman very comfortable with building an empire from the comfort of her own home. Martha Stewart would be a fabulous example of a Queen of Pentacles personality. Which means that it comes as no surprise when I read for female coaches and business women that this queen comes up every time we start to discuss money.

There is no doubt that the Queen of Pentacles has her money on her mind and her mind on her money. Perhaps there is something to be said about being firmly rooted in the earth. This queen knows only too well how situations can change without warning, and she will make sure that she has all she needs to weather any storm. It is apparent that the queen is in no rush, having slow and deliberate behavior, like all those in the suit of pentacles. For she truly understands that what is divinely, rightfully hers will be hers in its most perfect form in divine time and not a second before.

As an archetypal influence
The Queen of Pentacles prefers to put one foot in front of the other, all the while soaking up everything that particular step has to offer. Being present in each moment allows her the solid footing she needs, and it stops her from casting her concerns too far into the future. The Queen of Pentacles is

very aware that what happens today affects the outcomes of the tomorrow she is working to create.

Perhaps taking a lesson from her relaxed but attentive demeanor will serve you well. Just look at how calm she is in Llewellyn's Classic Tarot. Her throne sits under a newly budding tree as she lets her bare feet enjoy the outdoor air. She shows off her pentacle but we dare not try taking it from her. Without too much effort, this tranquil, relaxing scene could very quickly turn into a kung fu movie, complete with some kicks from her trusty bunny.

The Queen of Pentacles may not look like much of a warrior but will fight to protect what is hers and what she has built. This makes her a fierce queen and an overly protective mother. Like all the tarot queens, she does not take her duties and responsibilities lightly; she steps into her role with grace but never loses sight of her own wants, needs, desires, and dreams.

This is important, as far too often, women in particular allow themselves to be overwhelmed by duty. They put their own lives on hold so that they can attend to the needs of others. The Queen of Pentacles reminds you that this does not have to be the case. In fact, if you are grounded enough and stable on your own two feet, you can do both without even breaking a sweat. This does not mean you can have it all, all the time. But it does mean that with the Queen of Pentacles as your archetypal guide, you can live the life you desire by finding grace and harmony in the many hats you have chosen to wear.

As a spiritual influence

The Queen of Pentacles is a protector but does not smother; quite the opposite, really. The Queen of Pentacles is totally self-sustained and self-contained. She feels just as much at home alone in her garden as she does participating in one of the royal balls. It must be all of that down-to-earth, deeply grounded self-confidence. The comfortable self is very much portrayed in the Queen of Pentacles card from the Tarot of the Hidden Realm. We see her adorned with fall leaves reminiscent of harvest and in her hand an apple, yet another fertility symbol.

The connection here to harvest reminds us that what we sow we will reap. This queen is a magnificent gardener who is more than willing to give you some tips on how to grow the most amazing life out of your own manifestation garden. The apple connects us to the tree of life and all the wonders of the divine garden. It is as if the Queen of Pentacles was inspired by this verse of the Psalms:

> *Psalm 1:3–6: We need God's resources to bear fruit. But where we place our roots is paramount. Only as we grow them deeply into the spiritual resources of God's grace will we produce fruit.*

The Queen of Pentacles wants to invite you back to your divine garden. She wants to reconnect you with the fertile ground of your beginnings and show you how to plant the right seeds to ensure an ongoing supply. In many ways, she wants to be your connection to the divine so that you know exactly where to place your roots so you can tap directly into the spiritual source. As we know, a good and bountiful harvest means never having to worry about running out of food over the cold winter months—and like it or not, winter always comes.

So what have you sown? Will it be enough to get you through even the coldest of months? What could you grow more of? What seeds did you miss out on all together?

The Guardian of Earth in the Gaian Tarot continues on with this gardening theme and takes it to a grander scale. Here we see a farmer carry out the duties of the Queen of Pentacles. He is tending to his crops and making sure they are ready to harvest. Behind him we see stalks that have already passed their food-growing lives and are getting ready to return to the earth. Another important part of any garden is knowing when and where to harvest. Too soon will shorten the growing cycle of the plants, and too late will leave you with unusable results.

As a messenger

The Queen of Pentacles teaches us about due diligence. She reminds us that it's all well and good to know you can create what you need, but theory without committed action behind it will yield you nothing in return. It is important to know at all times what you have at your disposal and how you are going to use it. The Queen of Pentacles doesn't just sit on her royal ass and observe her garden, her home, her business, or her kingdom. She gets her hands dirty, tending to its health, expansion, growth, and prosperity.

She is no stranger to hard work and is more than willing to roll up her sleeves and get things done. Probably the best part about being a queen is not having to do it alone. The Queen of Pentacles has a supporting team who stands at the ready to assist her when she commands them.

What does your support team look like? Who do you have to hold you accountable to your health and wealth goals? How many skilled gardeners are you surrounding yourself with?

This queen's message is clear: do not forget to tap into that which made you, the earth. Send your roots deep into the soil and entangle yourself with Mother Earth energy. Let her support you as you grow, bloom, and bear fruit. Stretch toward Father Sky, and offer abundant blessings to those who stand beneath your branches. The Queen of Pentacles reminds us that our ability to create and manifest abundance in all its forms is a gift—a gift that is meant to be shared, not squandered.

Queen of Wands: Guardian of Fire

I could not, at any age, be content to take my place by the fireside and simply look on. Life was meant to be lived. Curiosity must be kept alive. One must never, for whatever reason, turn her back on life.

ELEANOR ROOSEVELT

Cardinal Fire
Zodiac: Aries
Keywords: Dynamic, competitive, seductive

As a person

If ever there were a firecracker in the tarot, the Queen of Wands would be it. This fiery Aries is a doer, not a complainer. She likes to put things in motion, get things done, and do it all with a bang. She is, after all, the Guardian of Fire. It is her job to nurture the element entrusted to her kingdom and that is the spark that keeps the whole suit of wands ablaze. This queen knows only too well how to create a passionate vibrant kingdom and also how to destroy it. I have no idea why, but when I think of someone who truly carries with her Queen of Wands energy, I always think of Beyoncé. She just seems to be the embodiment of this very powerful, very creative, very sensual energy.

The Queen of Wands is anything but shy about her power. She is fully energized and central to all the goings on in her court. This is one queen you won't see sitting still. She needs to move, to engage, and to inspire. As an aside, not all movement that she creates will be for her alone to carry through with. She will motivate others to action and get them moving toward their goals and dreams. She will also swallow you whole, burn you to pieces, and spit out your dust. She is a bit of a complicated woman with a bit of a temper. The words "Handle with Care" should probably be imprinted on her forehead.

Where the Queen of Wands in Llewellyn's Classic Tarot looks stern and somewhat defensive, the Queen of Wands in the Tarot of the Hidden Realm appears to be more cheerful and playful. There is no doubt that the Queen of Wands can be a lot of fun. She truly can be the bell of the ball and the light of the party. Just don't be fooled by this part of her personality. For she can change quickly from good-time party queen to "I'm going to destroy you and all you stand for," fiery vengeful queen in the blink of an eye. Fire is unpredictable and it can change directions so quickly that you don't even see it coming or know what hit you until it's too late.

As an archetypal influence

The Queen of Wands knows what she wants and she is not afraid to go and get it. She will do what needs to be done and won't take no for an answer. This queen is proud of who she is and what she has accomplished. This pride is evident in Llewellyn's Classic Tarot as we see the queen seated on a throne adorned with lions, the animal totem of pride. Next to her sits a black cat, a symbol of her fickle and sometimes egocentric ways. The blazing energy of the sun is shown in the sunflower she holds, and the solar headpiece of her throne. In her other hand she grips her wand.

The queen's animal totem, the cat, is generally selfish by nature. They come first, and then maybe if it serves them in some way, they will consider the needs and wants of those around them. It really does depend how the fires are burning in that particular moment. As an archetype this totem gives you permission to put yourself first when and where it is necessary. Coming in behind everyone else's needs does not have any advantages at all. So if you have trouble getting yourself together before you help others, the Queen of Wands and her feline companion are the perfect energy to work with.

The unpredictability of fire and feline energy also makes it harder for those around you to become complacent. Complacency is not a good energy to have around you if it is your job to lead, organize, or maintain any sort of power. Keep in mind that traditionally, the court was heavily dominated by men; any queen who was a ruler in her own right had to command respect and hold a fierce persona just to be taken seriously. Today we still see women having to stand their ground in order to be taken as seriously as their male counterparts. It is sad that we have not evolved much since feudal times, but it makes the queens in the tarot that much more important.

Yet despite all of this, the Queen of Wands is making her strong presence felt in today's world. Women and women's rights are front and center in the news again. This is because the time is ripe for the Queen of Wands in all women to stand her ground and demand what is rightfully hers: equal pay, exclusive rights to her own body, equal advancement in the workplace, paid maternity leave, and access to planned parenting, to name but a few human rights that really should never have had anything to do with gender.

As a spiritual influence

The suit of wands is not a suit I believe you can ever truly get on the right side of, mainly because it moves and shifts so frequently. You just have to take it for what it is, necessary and volatile. When it comes to dealing with this queen, respect is your best weapon. It is through working with the Queen of Wands that we learn how to become guardians of creative fire, not the owners. One cannot own fire; it is not something that can be bought and sold. It can however be tended to, nurtured, and respected. The keys of these lessons are shown in the Gaian Tarot. Although the gender of our queen changes with this card, the teachings and tools are the same.

Do you know how to light a good fire? One that will burn over an extended period of time? Do you even know what is the best combination of ingredients to feed your fire?

In order to light a fire, you will also need to have enough material to burn to sustain it. Fire requires a lot of energy to maintain, which is why many people find it hard to keep up with the Queen of Wands. In the Guardian of Fire card we see a nice fire burning on multiple logs inside a constructed fire pit. Our guardian is hunched over the flames, maybe to see where he needs more fuel or perhaps even to breathe life into reluctant flames. Fire also needs oxygen; it needs to breathe.

Standing watching over our guardian is a bobcat, yet another ode to the feline energy that is connected so strongly to this card and which to be honest can be very elusive in the wild. Yet like most mammals, this shy and often timid cat is drawn to the warmth the fire provides. Our guardian is also attentive enough to make sure the fire does not spread to where it is not required. Spreading fire is destructive fire and fire can spread very quickly when it is unattended and unsupervised.

Replace the word "fire" with any of the following words: "enthusiasm," "passion," "stamina," "creativity," "desire," "action," or even "power." Ask yourself if you have the right ingredients to sustain and grow the energy you are currently using. Then see if you are being attentive enough to know how to feed and nurture the energy. Are you distracted and disengaged and the energy has become unstable and destructive? In order to reap the rewards you are after, you will have to become the guardian and queen of your own fire.

As a messenger

Everything about this queen emulates power. Her throne is situated in what appears to be a barren landscape; nothing around her is growing, and there is no evidence of life beyond her throne. But here she sits and thrives. Even when conditions look harsh, she does not waver. For she understands that the spark of life itself resides within her and her kingdom. And if she so chooses, she will also be the force to destroy it. The Queen of Wands knows in every fiber of her being she is that powerful. This makes her the perfect archetype to work with if you want to get shit done. She will push you through your fears, set your doubts on fire, and will eat your excuses for breakfast.

Like all the queens in the tarot court, she can have compassion but she is not the queen you want to run to if you are having a pity party. She has no time and energy for coddling you or allowing you to indulge in egocentric apathy. She wants action. She wants to know what you are going to do, not how you feel about it. This is what makes the Queen of Wands a good coach but not much of a therapist. The Queen of Wands is all about the doing and not so much about the wooing. This again ties into that catlike energy she is often associated with. She is quick on her feet, flexible, and interested primarily in her own needs, desires, and wishes.

The Queen of Wands wants you to take action, but not just any action. She wants you to take focused, deliberate action toward something that not only serves you but everyone around you. An out of control, destructive life serves no one. But a deliberately creative and vibrant life is a spark worth spreading.

Queen of Swords: Guardian of Air

A strong woman understands that the gifts
such as logic, decisiveness, and strength are
just as feminine as intuition and emotional
connection. She values and uses all of her gifts.
NANCY RATHBURN

Cardinal Air
Zodiac: Libra
Keywords: Mediator, decisive, compassionate

As a person

Once upon a time I used to feel like this particular queen and
I were one and the same. We both operate from the mind first,
everything else later. Everything was a pursuit in intellectual

excellence. My mind was my weapon of choice and I would sharpen it daily. These days I notice I am more balanced in my approach to life and in general allow more of the other queens to permeate my energy. Not that there is anything wrong with being like the Queen of Swords. She will always be my personal default setting. But to be honest, it can be extremely exhausting living in her head 24/7 without a break or vacation.

The Queen of Swords is a demanding energy. She requires your full attention, all the time. This queen prides herself on her knowledge, logic, reasoning abilities, and intellectual prowess. She expects those around her to either keep up or shut up. The Queen of Swords has no tolerance for ignorance or stupidity. She takes ideas very seriously and no decision is ever entered into lightly.

Just like her alter ego, Justice, the Queen of Swords can see all sides of an argument or situation. Where possible, she will make the most logical, balanced, and rational decision. Just be warned that her ruling is final—she does not take kindly to those who do not agree with her very carefully thought-out solution. Real-life examples of the Queen of Swords would be the current women of the Supreme Court: Ruth Bader Ginsburg, Sonia Sotomayor, and Elena Kagan. If you have never heard these women rule, perhaps now would be a good time to dig up some of their transcripts.

As an archetypal influence

The sword the queen holds in Llewellyn's Classic Tarot is both literal and metaphorical. I am a firm believer in the literal action each card in the tarot gives us. To ignore its literal meaning would be, in my mind, only telling half the story. As we take a closer look at the Llewellyn's Classic card, we see the queen playfully caressing her substantial sword. As we learned with the Page of Swords, these weapons are not easy to wield and require a certain amount of strength and mastery. Although our queen is seated, she looks more than comfortable with that sword in her hand. So comfortable, in fact, that she really does look like she could spring forth at any moment and cut off someone's head. Do not let her air of peace fool you. She may very well wish to find peaceful solutions to difficult problems, but she is not above taking matters into her own hands to ensure she gets the result she desires. This queen knows quite well how to stand her ground and defend herself.

Metaphorically speaking, we can actually apply the lessons of strength and mastery to her other weapon of choice, her mind. The human mind may very well be a splendid thing, but if it is not trained correctly it can become weak, flabby, and highly impressionable. As the queen holds her sword across her body with the tip pointed to the heavens, we get the sense that she is letting us know she is armed in more ways than one. Her connection to the higher realms is hinted at by the angels and doves that decorate her throne. Doves have long been associated with the holy spirit and angels are the holy spirit's messengers.

The Queen of Swords not only feels she belongs within the higher realms, but she commands that all who come before her enter into it as well. Perhaps the butterfly that adorns the top of her throne hints at the transformation this particular queen offers. One could say that she offers transformation from the ego to the divine or perhaps liberates one from the emotional to the logical. It could also be that she frees us from a trapped, anxiety-ridden mind to the freedom of imagination and inspiration. Either way, she sits ready to make you an offer. The real question is, are you ready to receive what she is offering?

As a spiritual influence

The Queen of Swords asks the question "Where does creation begin?" For if in fact it does begin with consciousness, then our minds are the most powerful tool we have at our human disposal, making how we nurture our minds a top priority. This point of contemplation becomes evident in the Guardian of Air image from the Gaian Tarot, as she seems to be saying, "In the beginning there was sound." As the queen sits alone in the snow, she activates a singing bowl. Focused and controlled, she stills her mind and brings forth the vibrations of the universe. Who knows what sort of magical and miraculous things this sort of concentrated awareness will create.

Alone and isolated, the Queen of Swords's only companion are her thoughts. The ability to be alone and isolated is actually one of the queen's strong points. The ability to stand on one's own two feet and separate from everything else (even if for a little while) is a gift. The gift of solitude. Yet the Queen of Swords has no problem with her inner dialogue because she has learned that her mind is her greatest weapon, even on herself. The Queen of Swords reminds us that the mind—that is, our thoughts, beliefs, and inner dialogue—can make our physical experience seem like either heaven or hell on earth. Both of which start in your head and then manifest into the physical world around you.

The Queen of Swords in the Tarot of the Hidden Realm also looks contemplative, as if she is about to begin a ritual. Or maybe she has just finished, as it is hard to tell if she is taking her sword out of its protective cloth or putting it back in. This queen shows the importance of cleaning and protecting a sword or, to put it another way, keeping your thoughts clean and clear to protect your mind. By keeping her mental space protected and clutter-free, the queen honors her mind as a sacred space—a place of magic, power, imagination, and divinity.

As a messenger

Some people find this queen the coldest of all the court queens, as she doesn't exactly ooze comfort and warmth. Yet to me she is the only queen who can actually liberate you from the beliefs and mindsets that block the peace and comfort many desire to obtain. Let's face it, liberation is the key to transformation. One of the reasons this queen seems cold is that she has no time for excuses of any kind. She is, however, very dedicated to finding you a solution to any problem you bring before her.

It is vitally important that when this particular queen shows up in a reading, you understand that liking what she has to tell you is irrelevant. In fact, you need to work with her sword and separate yourself from your emotional mind so you can truly find the solution you seek. Keeping yourself bound to an answer that sounds like something you might like to hear will only keep you in a state of suffering. Let the Queen of Swords do her job and liberate you instead.

Attentive, thoughtful, and fully engaged is the Queen of Swords. When you stand before her, you will know without a shadow of a doubt that she heard you. It takes a strong person to be able to stand up for themselves over an extended period of time. Just as it takes strength to become comfortable with solitude and silence, as the mind starts to wander and talks endlessly to fill the void that separation creates. All of one's fears, doubts, regrets, and defeats start to creep in when things stay silent for long periods of time. In the silence there is nowhere to hide from yourself and there is nowhere to hide from the Queen of Swords.

Queen of Cups: Guardian of Water

To attribute to the Muse a special fondness for pain is to come too close to desiring and cultivating pain.
Wendell Berry

Cardinal Water
Zodiac Sign: Cancer
Keywords: Prophetic, creative, aware

As a person

The Queen of Cups is the most girly of our four tarot queens, well, in my opinion anyway. I mean, if ever there were a queen who loved to dress up and throw a wondrous feast or royal ball, it would be the Queen of Cups. The Queen of Cups is the most domestic of all the tarot queens, and much like the Queen of Pentacles, prefers to be home rather than out on the town. This could very well have something to do with the link between this card and the zodiac sign of Cancer, which is the most domestic sign in the zodiac. Cancer women in general are very house-proud; home and hearth play a big part in who they are. Cancer women will either open their homes up as places of comfort and celebration or they will fight to the death to keep the outside world out and keep their homes as sacred, safe sanctuaries for themselves and their loved ones.

The Queen of Cups does a similar thing with her personal space and royal court. As the queen grows, matures, and ages, how she uses space will change as well. Space is an interesting idea when it comes to dealing with this queen because water, her element, takes up space. It literally has the capacity to fill up anything that it can pour, leak, or flow into. Left unprotected, this water can become contaminated. No wonder this queen is so picky about what sort of energy she wants near her watery home.

Queen of Cups personalities are highly sensitive, are very creative, and wound easily. Believe it or not, the best example I can think of for Queen of Cups energy is the late Michael Jackson. He fits the Queen of Cups personality profile almost to a T. Ironically, I have actually come across more men who have this queen as a predominant energy than I have women. The late Robin Williams would be another example of this energy. Personable and highly sought after, the Queen of Cups prefers to be alone. People will very often confuse her social self for her real self. This is one of the downfalls of being as the water, always able to change that which is reflected on the surface.

As an archetypal influence

Constant flow and change are part of the element the Queen of Cups represents. Water can be open and expansive or small, intimate, and healing. In Llewellyn's Classic Tarot, we see the Queen of Cups resting comfortably in her seashell throne. The open ocean at her back, she dips her toe into what appears to be a protected inlet or cove on the beach. Perhaps there is wisdom in that toe dipping. Maybe her pose is letting you know the safest place to enter the water, the spot where the water is the calmest. Best not to jump all in when this card shows up in a reading. If the queen of water needs to dip her toe to check the safety of the undertow, perhaps you too could use a little caution.

The cup she holds in her hands is rather enormous and looks more like a trophy than a regular chalice. The size of this cup could allude to many things: the amount of life, love, and happiness she is willing to fill up on at any given time, or an indicator of a serious drinking problem. This queen may need a cup big enough for a whole bottle of wine, not just a polite glass. I am by no means saying that this queen is some sort of drunken lush; over the years, this card *has* come up when someone is a drunken lush or has one in the family. It is important to see this queen in both of her forms, light and empowered and shadowed and troubled. And the Queen of

Cups can and does sometimes represent a woman that likes to drown her sorrows and drink her emotions away.

This queen is highly sensitive. She feels everything. And I do mean everything. This sort of heightened emotional state can be overwhelming. So overwhelming in fact that a Queen of Cups out of power finds it almost impossible to get a grip on her sensitive state. The Queen of Cups out of power or reversed is a sign that she has not been able to master her incredible gift. This is in no way an excuse for addictive, destructive behavior; at some point she made a very conscious choice: learn to master her gifts and empower herself and all those around her, or sink into victim mode and abdicate all responsibility for her life.

The Queen of Cups has great intuitive powers and can be a force to be reckoned with. She is connected to both the Chariot and the Moon cards in the major arcana, which means she can be one hell of a mover and shaker, as well as an incredibly powerful shamanic visionary. For when this queen is tapped in and turned on, you think she can see right through to your very soul. The Queen of Cups makes things change very quickly. Just like the water she commands, her energy will make things flow, move, and churn. She can and does bring about massive waves of change. Change that will be both healing and beneficial for your spiritual and emotional well-being.

The Queen of Cups as healing archetype wants nothing more than to bring you into her arms during high tide and wash away your pain, sorrow, and suffering. When she is done with you, she will leave you on the beach during low tide healed, refreshed, and restored.

As a spiritual influence

Just like the moon, this queen will go through phases. There will be times when she is social and available to all, and then there will be times when she needs to be alone and sit in her own energy to do some deep contemplation and healing work. As long as this queen stays in power, the waning, darkening moon won't pull her under and tempt her with her vices. You may know people who have Queen of Cups tendencies, who seem to live their daily lives in phases, which to the untrained eye may seem inconsistent and somewhat bipolar. But the truth is, they are as predictable as the ocean tides to which they are linked.

This connection to the moon links the Queen of Cups to dreams and the land of the dreamtime. If you are trying to connect more with your dreamtime, meditation with the Queen of Cups will be of help. Use her as your guide and journey companion, as no one knows the land of the shadows better than this queen. Let the Queen of Cups support you as you express how you really feel about your goals, desires, and needs. Allow her to be the mirror you require to reflect back all of your fears, doubts, and inner blockages. Water is a reflective substance, after all. It doesn't matter if you like what is being reflected back to you, only that you see it and acknowledge it.

The Guardian of Water in the Gaian Tarot is the perfect card to use for reflective mirror work. She sits deep in the crystal clear ocean, yet with a movement of her hand she can change the images upon the surface. Take a look, if you dare, at the images this queen reveals. Dive deep into the reflection and allow yourself to see all that is inside your watery creative center. Let the queen shift the water to reveal what is holding you back and all that waits for you once you have cleared the way for it to flow into your life. Yes, the Queen of Cups is a complex woman. She is unpredictable yet cyclic, ever changing, yet perfectly still, just like the moon and water she is so intrinsically tied to. Then again, no one ever said it was easy being the queen.

This connection to the moon and the tides makes the Queen of Cups the perfect healing energy to work with when you feel you need to get back into the ebb and flow of life. She will guide you through the emotional undertow and lovingly place you in the moving currents of your life-giving waters.

As a messenger

The Queen of Cups always seems to know exactly what you need, even if you yourself seem to be protesting. She is highly intuitive and can read people like a book. Whatever you do, don't try to lie to her, because she is not listening to a single word you say. Instead, she is reading your energy. And it is telling her everything she needs to know about who you are and how you operate. When she shows up in a reading, she is answering the question you should have asked—not the one you did ask.

The gaze of the Queen of Cups in the Tarot of the Hidden Realm alludes somewhat to this inner knowing as the queen appears to be looking right through the viewer. The smirk on her face lets you know that trying to hide, lie, or pull the wool over her eyes won't work. She has your number and is not afraid to call it. This ability to size people up allows her to create quite a powerful inner circle and support team, as the Queen of Cups knows quite well how to nurture and foster the innate gifts and talents of others.

So where are your gifts and talents? How are you supporting them emotionally? What fears, doubts, and blocks are you allowing to stop you from truly stepping into your gifts?

What sort of healing would you like the Queen of Cups to assist you with?

The Queen of Cups really does have an eye for extraordinary talent and beautiful things. So if she has shown up in your reading or daily draw, she considers you extraordinary as well.

Connecting Exercises and Spreads

The queens show us in a multitude of ways how we see, feel, and harness power. Whether you see yourself as queen—wife of the king or queen—female king is important, as women in general are not taught to ask for power nor are many trained in keeping it. This makes the four tarot queens incredibly important, for each of them can act as mother, sister, teacher, and guide on your journey to your divine power. Some of us already know which areas of our lives we feel confident and strong in and which ones we tend to shy away from or avoid like the plague. But sometimes our perception is not what it seems. Working with each of the four queens over an extended period of time will let you know for sure just where your strengths and weaknesses lie.

When we talk about "power," I don't mean dominating anyone or becoming a heartless asshole; none of those things illustrate real power. Real power is calm, quiet, unassuming, and a force to be reckoned with all the same. Real power is, for lack of a better way to express it, a vibe. It's an energy that oozes from every part of your being: confidence, self-worth, self-respect, compassion, understanding, and decisive action taking. Really powerful people know when to sit still and when to take action. They know how to make difficult decisions and how to live with the consequences of those decisions. Power can be mundane, invisible, and yet its presence is felt by all those who come in contact with it. So where is your power and how are you using it?

Pick one of the four tarot queens to work with over the next seven days. I recommend starting with the one you feel the most out of power with; for example, perhaps you lack confidence and feel unable to assert yourself or your thoughts and feelings. Think about working with the Queen of Wands because one thing this queen is not is shy! Or maybe you don't feel you trust your intuition, or get easily emotionally overwhelmed. Work with the Queen of Cups. For mental discipline or expanded awareness, the Queen of Swords is your mentor and for health, well-being, and money, the Queen of Pentacles is your manifestation guru.

Keep your queen's card somewhere you can see it while you are working together and start your morning together with a focused five-minute meditation. Hold the card and look at your queen, focus your breathing, and just sit with her for five minutes. You can light a candle or play some music if you want, but I really recommend silent meditation. This way you can open yourself up for a dialogue with the queen or just be receptive of any messages that might come through as you breathe and stay focused and connected to your queen. End your session by visualizing the two of you becoming one and the same person. You can then draw another card from your tarot deck to add to the energy or build on any messages you may have gotten while in meditation.

I understand that five minutes doesn't seem like a long time, but you will be amazed at how many people will struggle to keep their focus even for this long. I have been teaching meditation classes for over seven years now, and it never ceases to amaze me how many people start to fidget after only thirty seconds! So if you can stay fully focused and present for the whole five minutes of this exercise, you and your queen will get along just fine.

Make sure you have a way to track this work, be it in a journal, Word document, or blog. Write down your journey with each queen and see just how much she changes your day-to-day experience.

Four Queens and an Empress Spread

Earlier in this book I discussed briefly that the four tarot queens can actually be viewed as the four inner bodies or archetypes of the Empress. The Empress of the tarot empire is the pinnacle of feminine energy and the embodiment of the sacred feminine. In this spread, the Empress acts as your significator card and the four tarot queens will be the elements that make her whole. They are her emotional, mental, physical, and spiritual bodies and in this spread they also become yours. This spread is useful if you are feeling out of balance or you have a client who may wish to explore themselves a little deeper.

To do this spread you will first need to remove the Empress and the four tarot queen cards from your deck. Place them in the position marked out in the following diagram:

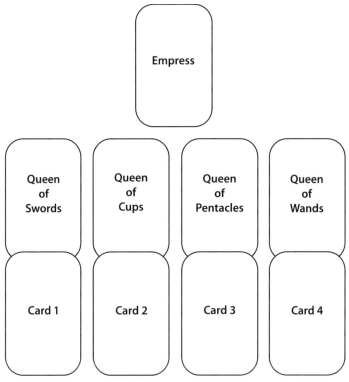

Four Queens and an Empress Spread

Pick up the remaining cards in your tarot deck and give them a good shuffle. Next you are going to select four cards that will be placed on top of the four tarot queens.

Empress

Queen of Swords   Queen of Cups   Queen of Pentacles Queen of Wands

10 of Swords   Ace of Pentacles   3 of Cups   The World

Four Queens and an Empress Spread (Sample Reading)
(Llewellyn's Classic Tarot)

- *Card 1/Queen of Swords*—The card that shows up here tells the story of your mental body. It shows how you are currently processing information and whether your mind is clear, focused, and engaged. This card will offer tips and action steps. In the example above, we see the 10 of Swords over the Queen of Swords. Something you have been churning over or hanging on to has to go. It is literally dead information and is blocking new and useful data from coming your way.

- *Card 2/Queen of Cups*—This card lets us see the condition of the emotional or creative body. This card will reveal how well you are currently processing your feelings and emotions and if they are moving you forward or drowning you. In our working example we see the Ace of Pentacles. What a lovely card to have here, as it shows the opportunity for expansion, growth, and healing. When an ace comes along, it always offers up a new beginning

- *Card 3/Queen of Pentacles*—The card represents the physical body of the Empress—or more to the point, you. Remember that in this reading, you are the Empress. This card gives you clues to how your body is doing. If any one of the more troubling cards shows up here, please do not panic. It is merely a reference and guide to assist you not to condemn you. In our example we see the 3 of Cups. Hooray, you have cause for celebration! Allow your body the chance to relax, have fun, and hang out with friends.

- *Card 4/Queen of Wands*—In this spread, the Queen of Wands becomes the spiritual or divine body. She represents our connection to our higher selves and how we see ourselves in relation to the sacred feminine energy that runs through us. In our example reading we see the World. What a fascinating card to have in this position. The World shows that we have attained the perfect conditions to be, do, or have whatever we want. It can mean that the world is in your hands.

Wrapping this spread up, we could say that despite the mind being distracted with information that doesn't serve it, the Empress self is pretty balanced and healthy. Opportunity and celebration are at hand while the world is there for the taking!

Go ahead, give this spread a try. It is a lot of fun and can be extremely helpful.

The Kings

Uneasy lies the head that wears a crown.

WILLIAM SHAKESPEARE

. . . .

In this chapter we will look at the many roles and functions the four kings of the tarot empire play, as they are not just kings—they are leaders, elders, and the last stop along the path of each of their suits. Once you journey from ace to king, there is nowhere else for you to go, which means the four kings of the tarot empire are also ending cards. They represent the end of a cycle, a journey, or path of learning. Eventually we all have to step out of the shadows of the student and pick up the robe of the master. This is where the four kings of the tarot will assist you. For they know only too well what it means to carry the burden of mastery.

History, Myth, and Legend

In our very modern world, we are very much removed from the kings of the Middle Ages, so much so we tend to fantasize about opulent courts with kings doing nothing but throwing banquets, womanizing, and indulging themselves in their basest of desires. To be fair, the courts of the eighteenth century were a bit like this, but not quite the orgy of the senses that we often see on both the big and small screen. This level of opulence was short-lived and very much at the end of royal and regal power, however. Kings of the early Middle Ages had it much more difficult. In fact, being king was a brutal and bloody occupation. Kings were forged in battle and the battles were endless. Not to mention that there was always someone else wanting your crown, your land, and your army. To be king you had to be strong, fit, agile, and a fearless warrior above all. Kings may have been the most powerful men in their kingdom, but they were also the ones with the biggest targets on their backs, meaning they had the least amount of freedom. How ironic that the most powerful man in the land is also the most vulnerable.

Just think for a minute how much energy these kings actually put into holding on to their titles. Everything they did was to retain and expand their power. Sometimes this power was for the greater good of all involved but sometimes it was just egocentric and purely selfish. The kings of the Middle Ages had to fight morning, noon, and night to keep what most later kings took for granted as their birthright. In this respect, the kings have much to teach us about commitment, power, focus, discipline, and determination.

The kings teach us that the right to lead is earned, not given. And once you have it, there is no guarantee you will keep it—unless of course you are willing to fight for it. For a king to give up, give in, or stop trying meant death, torture, or complete and utter ruin. I wonder how much more seriously we would take our decisions if these were the only options we were given. Makes you wonder, doesn't it?

To be a king, one has to have more than just royal blood in his veins. A king needs a desire to expand, grow, and unite as many people as possible. Over time, this vision can become blurred by an increase of power. Yet most kings (not all) start with a clear vision of what sort of mark they wish to leave on the world. This can be seen with some of the more famous kings in history

- *Alexander III, aka Alexander the Great* (reigned 336 BCE–323 BCE), established one of the largest empires in the ancient world and built twenty cities all bearing his name. To accomplish this, Alexander spent the majority of his reign on a never-ending military campaign, killing, exterminating, and overthrowing countries, governments, and religions.

- Kings like *Offa of Mercia* (reigned 757 CE–796 CE) were just as much opportunists as warriors. Offa seized power after a lengthy and bloody civil war. After a few more hostile takeovers, beheadings, and strategic marriages, Offa was said to be one of the most powerful rulers of Anglo-Saxon England. However, his authority was never stable nor ever went without some form of revolt or challenge.

- *Genghis Khan* (reigned 1206 CE–1227 CE) was able to unite almost all of the nomadic tribes of northeast Asia during his rule, under one Mongol Empire. He established one writing system for the empire and was able to teach religious harmony by practicing religious tolerance. He was also able to bring order and political cohesion to the Silk Road trading route. That said, this all came with a price—a very bloody one.

There is no doubt that all three of these men changed the course of history, but some could argue that the price that was paid for this change may not have really been worth the so-called reward. Even though kings today don't have the same amount of power they once had, we still have men fighting over land, wanting to expand territories, and not really caring about how many rivers of blood they create in the process. The title may no longer be the same, but the quest for power still seems to shape the world in which we live, making the four kings of the tarot court just as important today as they were when they were first created.

Yet despite the brutal history our past kings have left us with, there is hope. And that hope comes from one of the most famous kings of all, King Arthur. Sure, he is fictional; no one can actually prove that Arthur really existed outside of the pages of poems and folklore, but he is the king of true imagination: a king of honor, a king for the people, deeply connected to the place from which he was created. Arthur promises something no real king seemed to be able to deliver—magic, romance, and a happy ending. Arthur was the hero no living person could every possibly be, which is why today Arthurian legends burn so bright and inspire so many. Which of our four tarot kings matches up to this sort of legacy? Well, that's really up to you, for only you know what it is you are looking for in a heroic king.

The kings of the tarot not only carry with them all of the history that came before them but also connect to myth, legend, and folklore. They also bring with them the possibility of what leadership can look like in the future. The three decks we will explore in this chapter show the kings in three very different ways, including the possibility of a female king, suggesting that gender and leadership don't have to be inexorably linked. The four kings of the tarot are leaders in their own kingdoms, which is important, as leadership does tend to be localized. The lesson of taking care of your own kingdom first is a lesson many politicians could learn. For now, let's focus on your personal kingdom.

King of Cups: Elder of Water

You can't cross the sea merely by
standing and staring at the water.
RABINDRANATH TAGORE

Fixed Water
Zodiac Sign: Scorpio
Keywords: Intensity, depth, rebirth

As a person

The King of Cups is the ruler of the watery world of the south; summer is his favorite time of year. Our king is an emotional guy and he has been known to get swept up in the emotional waves of his own creating. This king is a feeling king; sometimes he feels too much and it overwhelms him and sometimes he feels nothing at all. He is a Scorpio with Libra tendencies, which tends to make him cynical but fair. He is a caring father most of the time. He loves deeply, but that doesn't mean he is a good husband. The King of Cups can be emotionally self-indulgent and extremely manipulative. Even though he believes in justice, he prefers it when it is in his favor.

In this respect, I find the King of Cups much like Henry VIII. Wildly creative, a lover of beauty, art, and the higher workings of the mind, yet his kryptonite was women and booze. He possessed both the positive qualities of this card and the less desirable ones as well. Henry enacted great and longlasting changes, some of which we still benefit from. This is the deep legacy of the King of Cups. He desires to leave a mark on the world, one that will last long after he is gone. Not all kings are this forward thinking.

The King of Cups from Llewellyn's Classic Tarot is a reminder of the kings from Henry's day: stiff, sullen, and somewhat smug. This king looks like he would rather smash you over the head than offer you a drink. I know a few people who are just like this. They like to let you know they are in control but then want to make you feel included. Can you relate?

There is no doubt that a King of Cups personality is a tricky one to deal with, especially considering he is just as changeable as water, the element he has mastered. One day he might be the most giving, inspiring, and endearing man to be around…and the next he is moody, cold, and extremely distant.

As an archetypal influence

The king is often seen with a large chalice in his hand, and a lot of times it is illustrated as being full. Yes, the King of Cups can be a drunk—and a mean one, at that. For the most part, however, he stays on an even keel. Perhaps this has to do with this age. This king is older and wiser, and he has learned life's most difficult and challenging lessons. Because of his deeply emotional core, this king's greatest weakness is love, for he tends to follow his heart more than he follows his head. And when his heart leads him astray, his head will push him to the darkest parts of his emotional being.

There is no doubt that when this king loves, he does so from the very depths of his being. The King of Cups's love is not always directed at just one person, however, nor is it limited to people. He can be deeply in love with his work, his power, his need for knowledge, or anything else that this king becomes passionate about. Sir Richard Branson embodies this beautifully. There is no better example of a true heart-centered leader. Just like the King of Cups, Branson loves being surrounded by creative, flowing energy. How he has set up his companies and how he runs (or more to the point, *doesn't* run) his teams is the holy grail of business legend. If you ever wanted an entrepreneurial archetype for human-based businesses of the twenty-first century, look no further than Branson.

If we look at the King of Cups from the Tarot of the Hidden Realm, he really could be a young Richard Branson (minus the facial hair). He is deeply emotive and we can see he is a sensitive and feeling leader just by his eyes. Sir Richard Branson has been known to cry in public on more than one occasion, showing that he is not afraid to exhibit emotion and vulnerability, one of the more admirable traits of the King of Cups in power.

As a spiritual influence

If we look at the court cards as a continuum, we would have to acknowledge the kings as the last step, or—more to the point—the last point of expansion of the suit itself. In this case, the King of Cups would be the last point of awakening along the path of cups. When you get to the king, you have come to an ending. But with all endings are also beginnings. Everything you have learned from the page to the queen comes together in this card. So what's left to learn on this watery journey? Why, how to continue the cycle of life, of course.

Without the element of liquid water, there is no life. We know this as a very real scientific fact, as scientists have spent decades looking for planets with liquid water on them in hopes of finding both new life and a potential new planet for human habitation. Without water, we have nothing— no hope, no new beginnings, and no chance of rebirth. The King of Cups holds all three of these hopes in the palms of his hands. He wants to show you how to master this element in such a way that when things come to a natural ending, they transform into the vortex that will create the new birth chamber for the potential lying in wait with the Ace of Cups.

This may all sound like the queen's job, but in actuality, it can't be, for she is not the ending point of the suit. The queen instead helps you clean the waters and prepare them for this final stage. She holds up the mirror to your desires and doubts, and assists you in preparing to let go. The king then steps in to finish up where the queen left off. He is now your guide on the final leg of your journey.

As a spirit guide, this card has much to show, share, and teach you. Just understand that in his domain, he is king and you are there because he allows it to be so. Honor this and your time with the King of Cups, and he could change the course of your life and how you move through the world.

So what in your life is coming to an end? What mark do you wish to leave on the world? What things do you love with every fiber of your being? And how will you set up the conditions for a wondrous rebirth into the divine potential of the aces?

These above questions are more points of meditation than anything else. They should not be answered impulsively. The King of Cups does not like to stay on the surface—he likes to dive into things. When he has showed up in your reading, you should join him in his journey to the deep waters of answers and solutions.

As a messenger

The King of Cups can have one of two messages for you when he graces your reading or daily draw with his watery presence. He could indeed be showing up as an actual leader, someone whose shoes you need to walk in to meet a goal, fulfil a dream, or grant a wish. Or he may be guiding you to your next point of expansion. Either way, you can rest assured movement will be involved.

The question you ask will give you an idea which persona he is effecting. If you asked a business or career question, there is a good chance he has shown up to talk about leadership styles and possibly even question your love for what you do. If you asked about your relationship, then you need to first establish who the king actually is in the reading. Is he you or the person you are asking about? Then and only then will the other cards around the king let you know what his message is for you.

If you are asking more regular life questions, there is a very good chance this king has shown up to guide you out of one cycle into the next. He probably knows which current to ride to get you to where you want to go faster. Just hold on to your stomach because it won't be a slow and comfortable ride. The key to this king is in the question you ask. Pay attention to what words you have used, and let the King of Cups guide you into the flow of the answer you seek.

King of Pentacles: Elder of Earth

The ultimate measure of a man is not where
he stands in moments of comfort, but where he
stands at times of challenge and controversy.
Martin Luther King Jr.

Fixed Earth
Zodiac sign: Taurus
Keywords: Steady, reliable, grounded

As a person

Everything about this king screams "plenty." Just take a look at
the image of the King of Pentacles in Llewellyn's Classic Tarot,
from the lush garden he sits in to the two bulls on his throne.
Even the grapes on his cloak reek of abundance. He sits atop

his throne, satisfied with what he has accomplished thus far. Do not be fooled, however—he is not necessarily finished or has stopped creating abundance, as this king makes money in his sleep. Think about men like Warren Buffet and Bill Gates or a woman like Oprah Winfrey. These three real-life examples are typical King of Pentacles personalities. They are so tapped and tuned in to the vibration of supply that they can't even give their money away faster than it comes in. Each and every year they give more money away than most people will even see in a single lifetime. Yet despite this, it just keeps coming back to them tenfold. Sometimes it's hard to be king of the material world!

The queen of this suit may be the nurturer and power networker, but the King of Pentacles bears the full weight and responsibility of his kingdom squarely on his own shoulders. This king is not just the master of his element but is the elder and leader of all physical supply for his realm. He knows only too well what goes in and what goes out of his kingdom. He knows where there has been excess and where there has been limited resources. Try as you might, you cannot lie to or fool this king. Just as we saw with the Queen of Pentacles, the king's throne is placed outdoors, in the garden. Behind him is all he has built and all he protects.

The King of Pentacles is grounded and deliberate with words, thoughts, and actions. Very rarely would he be compulsive or reactionary. He understands that everything comes in its own time, and he finds comfort in cyclic experiences, for the King of Pentales understands the rhythm, the flow, and the order of the natural world in which he lives. He knows it is better to wait for the best conditions than to rush into something half-assed. The ability to wait things out and allow things time to grow may very well be his secret weapon.

Taurus men are incredibly stubborn (think of the term "bull-headed") so it may be a little easier for him than others to not give up until he breaks through to what he desires. Yet that determination is a habit, and habits can be learned and adapted by anyone, even those not used to sticking with things and seeing them through. "Finish what you started" is this king's motto.

As an archetypal influence

The King of Pentacles is also the patriarch of the family; he is the father or possibly even grandfather to all those in his element. This relationship is beautifully illustrated in the King of Pentacles card from the Tarot of the Hidden Realm. I don't know why but this king always reminds me of Father Christmas, the father or grandfather to not just a select few children but to all. The love, affection, gentleness, and innocence that radiates from this card makes me want to also feel the comfort and safety this king brings to the child that he cradles in his arms.

This strong yet gentle patriarch stands under the holly holding his most precious treasures. In this respect we are all reminded that there is more to life than just "stuff," and abundance reaches far beyond our bank accounts. This version of the father of the earth helps bring us back to reality. Here we may ground all of our illusions of grandeur and remind ourselves why we are really building strong, secure, and stable lives. We don't just do it to benefit ourselves, even though we absolutely should. We do it to benefit as many as possible, especially those we hold the closest to our hearts.

How often are you impatient with your goals? How often do you find yourself chasing money? How often do you say "this is taking too long"?

In today's fast-paced world, the King of Pentacles reminds us that there are no real overnight successes. He also stands as proof positive that nothing happens in a vacuum. Time, effort, focus, and good old-fashioned hard work will get you all you desire. To this king, rolling up your sleeves and getting your hands dirty is real, valuable hard work. Additionally, he wants you to have the will to never give up, which brings us to some very important rules regarding abundance: clutter, loose ends, and procrastination.

It is very hard to create when surrounded by a lot of clutter, loose ends, unfinished work, half-baked ideas, and offers and solutions that were never followed up on. This does not create abundance. This often creates confusion and uncertainty, which lead to procrastination, leading to a cycle of inaction. How anyone thinks they can create a never-ending supply out of nonaction is truly beyond comprehension. The King of Pentacles knows only too well that you must always follow through, you tie up loose ends as quickly as possible, and you give away whatever is no longer relevant or necessary for what you are working to create. If you truly want to get the inside story on the law of attraction, the King of Pentacles is your man.

If this king is out of power, reversed, or blocked in, be prepared for a totally different king. The King of Pentacles out of power can be a real asshat. He can use his money to manipulate those around him, to get what he wants, when he wants it. He can also go from welcoming to closed off and cold. When this king is out of power, he has no interest in anyone but himself and what he can take. He will shut down and become paranoid about what he has, suspicious of whomever he thinks is trying to take it away from him. Not to mention he will withdraw from social engagements and offer advice to no one. When the King of Pentacles is out of power or reversed, he has forgotten who he is and all the reasons he was given the gift of supply in the first place.

As a spiritual influence

The image of the spinner in the Gaian Tarot reminds us that all these kings are gender-fluid; one does not necessarily need to be male to be a patriarch of the earth. In fact, this card asks some very important questions about what it means to be a leader and elder. If we think of the king sitting at the top of the pentacles court, the Elder of Earth asks, "What does it mean when you have reached the top? What happens when there is nowhere else for you to go?"

The King of Pentacles has reached the pinnacle of his suit; there is nowhere else for him to ascend, yet his fate is still very much in his own hands. He may not be able to go up, but he sure can go down. The Elder of Earth card shows us in a not-so-subtle way that all that once was can be changed and turned into something else. Everything can be repurposed; nothing stays the same.

Kings can and do get overthrown. Fathers can leave, die, or not even be in the picture at all. CEOs can be fired and replaced—everything you have built can be taken away or come crashing down around you. To be the king of supply may be easy, but staying there is hard and vigilant work. But perhaps it's just as well—this king likes to roll his sleeves up and take one step at a time, no matter how many times he has to repeat the process.

As a messenger

The King of Pentacles understands material wealth so well that he cannot help but keep swelling in the vortex of supply. He is what he attracts. If we cut to the chase, the King of Pentacles is a moneymaking fool! Yet the king in Llewellyn's Classic Tarot looks very approachable. He really does look like he wants to share his secrets of success with you. Will you take the king up on his offer? Will you come sit at his throne in his garden and listen to what he has to say?

Or do you feel you already know all there is to building, creating, and maintaining wealth and abundance?

Remember, this king can teach about all forms of physical abundance including health. Health is one of the biggest resources this king has, for how can one lead and rule if one is stressed out and sickly? He knows that one cannot create and build if one is always laid up in bed with one complaint or another.

The King of Pentacles has a wealth of knowledge to share, yet he won't share it with just anyone. He may give words of advice and perhaps offer a solution here and there, but he is really looking for a student, an apprentice, or someone to train and mold. He doesn't want to make someone else in his likeness, necessarily, but the person must have similar values, understanding, and beliefs.

Will it be you? Will you allow the King of Pentacles to show you the next step once you have reached the end of the pentacles path?

Think about it this way: making money, gaining success, and obtaining health is one matter, but keeping it is quite another. No one knows this better than the King of Pentacles.

King of Swords: Elder of Air

In a battle between two ideas, the best one doesn't necessarily win. No, the idea that wins is the one with the most fearless heretic behind it.
Seth Godin

Fixed Air
Zodiac sign: Aquarius
Keywords: Idealistic, assertive, determined

As a person

The King of Swords is master of the mind. He is not just able to have fabulous ideas, but he is also able to stay present and focused to see all of his ideas come to fruition, which is astonishing when we consider that most of his ideas, concepts, and creative imaginings seem to be advanced or before their time. The King of Swords in many respects is a visionary; he sees things others cannot yet comprehend. He can spot a trend before it begins and can predict a need before it even exists. How does he do it? He constantly shifts his perspective. Although this king may be a fixed air sign, his mind is unlimited, fluid, and lucid. The fixed nature of his sign allows him the mental discipline he needs to stick with an idea, concept, or belief. The sword is double-edged, after all. Once this king has set his mind to something, it is virtually impossible to change his mind or sway him from his path...unless it was his own idea, of course.

The King of Swords from the Tarot of the Hidden Realm looks like he knows all about the responsibility associated with the sword he carries next to him. Unlike the king in Llewellyn's Classic Tarot, this version of the King of Swords looks completely lost in contemplation, almost troubled. To me at least, he looks less inviting and would be offended if you were to try and break his concentration. The look of deep contemplation could let us know that right now he is taking his time, mulling things over in a form of meditation. Either way, this particular King of Swords is hard to read, an actual personality trait of some King of Swords people.

It is not uncommon for leaders to keep what they know to themselves, under wraps and away from the prying eyes of those who want to see the king fall from his throne. It is this sort of mental mastery that allows King of Swords personalities to maintain their power and lead with confidence. Just like a good poker player, the King of Swords keeps his plans of takeovers, advancements, and mergers close to his chest. But even the best poker player has a tell, and for this king, it is his sword: how he holds it, where he places it, and how close it is to his physical body will give you some clues as to how he will use it. For your part, you will know whether or not you should come closer or stand clear.

In real-life we see examples of the King of Swords in people like Nikola Tesla and Steve Jobs. Think about it: more than a hundred years later, we are still trying to catch up with Tesla's visionary ideas; who knows what incredible Jobs's ideas Apple has locked away for the future? Only time will tell. And that is the legacy of the King of Swords.

As an archetypal influence

When this king is in power, fear and doubt have no place in his court—he is determined, confident, and fully engaged. This is the image we see in Llewellyn's Classic Tarot, an open and receptive leader. He may have his ridiculously long sword beside him, but he hardly looks ready to grab it and launch into battle. If anything, it looks like his sword is more a point of concentration, the physical thing that keeps him tethered to the earthly plane. Let's face it, sometimes we can all get very lost inside our heads. And it is not hard to get caught up and swept away in our dreams or our fears. The king's sword may be a key or clue to what you need if you feel yourself struggling to stay focused and on task—a physical anchor. If this card shows up in a reading, it might be a good idea to see if you have a touchstone in place to ground and focus your mental energy. So what is your personal touchstone and how does its physical presence keep you grounded and present?

Mental energy needs to be grounded if it is to be of use. Otherwise it gets confused, tainted, or lost altogether. The King of Swords knows this all too well, which is why he makes sure he can always follow a thought to its logical conclusion. The ability to draw ideas out of our heads is what journal work is all about. It is a physical way to take out of the mind what is not necessary or important for greater work or a goal as well as flashes of inpsiration and brilliance that just happen to show up in that moment. As a writer and someone who very much lives in my head, I know only too well how important it is to keep the mind flowing. I do a journal exercise every single morning to dump out anything and everything that could block my creative mental energy. This allows me to stay focused on my daily writing tasks and makes sure my mind doesn't wander off to think about things that are irrelevant to the task at hand. Once my morning mind dump is completed, I no longer have extra noise in my head.

Due to their unparalleled vision, it is not uncommon for King of Swords personalities to feel out of place in the time period they exist in. They can become isolated, alone, and disengaged with the outside world. This disconnection to time and space can easily turn into depression or a form of permanent distraction. When this happens, our King of Swords goes from in power to out of power. This can show up in a reading as a reversed card or an upright king card surrounded by other reversed or blocked cards.

So what happens when a brilliant mind gets turned upside down? Nothing good is the short answer. The brain truly is a mysterious thing and even with all of our scientific and medical advancements, we still know so little about it or what it is capable of. We do however know that the brain does give us clues to our state of well-being by the way it processes information. Different areas light up in the brain when we are happy, sad, anxious, excited, or stressed. Some of this energy is stronger than others, and some of it even turns the data we receive around so that it keeps us in the same state we were in when we received it. If the King of Swords finds himself out of power, you can be sure that his brain is not processing data the same way it would if he was in power, flowing, and riding the visionary wave. Instead, our king would be distracted, impatient, irrational, forgetful, and paranoid. Where he was once so careful with his words, thoughts, and beliefs, he is now rude, blunt, scattered, and incomprehensible.

As a spiritual influence

The king is not just a leader of his kingdom, he is also the patriarch of his family and the elder of his element. I do find it interesting that the Elder of Air card in the Gaian Tarot shares the same butterfly motif as the King of Swords in Llewellyn's Classic Tarot. The butterfly is the totem of transformation, liberation, and alchemy. From a spiritual perspective, these are exactly the things the King of Swords offers all of those who are brave enough to come before him. He offers the chance to transform your thoughts, beliefs, and words. He has the ability to liberate you from the supposed limitations of the physical world by offering you a broader, more expansive view of who you are and your capabilities. What we think, say, and believe creates the world we experience. The King of Swords teaches you how to set the most supportive and creative vibration for your goals, dreams, and desires. He will instruct you on how to set your vibrational energy so you can better control what you attract and repel. The king also knows that his level of awareness is a learned skill that takes time to master. Luckily for you, he is the master; if you ask nicely and approach respectfully, he will show you too.

As a messenger

You hear the term "thought leader" thrown around all the time in coaching circles, but what does it really mean? What does a thought leader truly look like? That sort of person looks like the King of Swords, of course! The thoughtful, articulate master of air, the King of Swords is the perfect archetype of a thought leader in any industry.

Here the King of Swords offers us up the key to being a master thought leader: keep your mind flowing. How exactly are you doing this?

The King of Swords knows well when to let something go so something more beneficial can flow through. His mental feelers are constantly scouting the energy around him for more information, new ideas, and expanded points of being. It is not uncommon for this king to start with a concept that is so far out there and mold it into a concept that is highly valued and regaled. This is the mastery of his vision, making this king the perfect confidant for your biggest, craziest, scariest dream, wish, or goal. The King of Swords has the ability to take that desire and break it down into logical, rational pieces. He can show you where to place your focus and how to steel your mind against doubt and fear.

King of Wands: Elder of Fire

Leadership is an action, not a position.
Donald McGannon

Fixed Fire
Zodiac sign: Leo
Keywords: Inspiring, explosive, charismatic

As a person
A fixed fire sign in the house of Leo, the King of Wands sits on his throne in the barren lands of his eastern kingdom. The energy of the lion looms large over him, almost as a protective

guide in Llewellyn's Classic Tarot. This makes the king less than approachable, although he does have a bit of a reputation as being overly confrontational. Some might even call him brash or even downright rude.

The King of Wands has an intense energy about him that makes you want to approach with caution. All the same, his manner doesn't seem to stop people who feel drawn to his magnanimous energy. Like moths to a flame, people can't stop flocking to the feet of this particular king. Yet just like the lion, you never quite know if he is going to play with you, dominate you, or kill you. You might think that sounds harsh, but fire is one of the harshest elements.

If there was ever a poster child for adult ADHD, it would be the King of Wands. He just can't sit still and finds no delight whatsoever in watching time and life pass by. You won't find the King of Wands standing on the sidelines of anything. He is either right in the middle of the action or he *is* the action. I pity the fool who thinks he can take him on. Yet just like the lion, there are those who try their hand at challenging this king for all he has. Others see the power, fame, and fortune this king has amassed and think they would like it as their own. As we have established, it's really not easy being king. And unfortunately for the King of Wands, he wears one of the biggest targets on his back in the entire tarot empire.

King of Wands personalities may be volatile, but they can also be fearlessly protective and faithful. Win the heart of this king and you will have a protector for life. As the last stop in the suit of wands, he has earned his right to his throne. If ever there were a king forged in the heat of battle, it would be the King of Wands. Just look at the King of Wands from the Tarot of the Hidden Realm—he is the picture of a battle veteran. And it is during those long battles that his bonds would have also been forged with those around him. This king's affection may not be easily earned, but once you have it, know that it will be as intense as the energy this king has sworn to protect.

People with King of Wands energy are charismatic, charming, and unpredictable. They tend not to care about what others think of them, nor do they even bother governing their words and actions. I hate to admit it, but Donald Trump makes a perfect King of Wands—you love to hate him and hate to love him. That is the same sort of feeling one has about the fiery elder of wands. Like it or not, they get shit done, regardless if those around them are not at all impressed with the process. It is oftentimes hard to argue with the end results. But then again, that is typical fire, never a thought for the path it created to get to where it needed to go.

As an archetypal influence

Fire spreads and destroys without conscience or regret. It just burns. So too does the King of Wands. He burns with all the power, strength, and desire of all the warrior kings that came before him. He has a massive vision and will do what it takes to make it happen. This king is all about the action. Just take a look at where the flame of his crown sits in Llewellyn's Classic Tarot card: right on top of his third eye.

Mistake? Coincidence? I think not.

The King of Wands burns brightly with ambition and desire. He wants it all and he wanted it yesterday. There is no doubt in his mind whatsoever that he is entitled to everything he wants and then some. In and of itself, it is probably not a bad characteristic for a leader and ruler to have, but what about the cost?

This is a question the King of Wands poses in a reading. He asks: what cost can you live with? Where do you draw the line? How much is too much?

The King of Wands is set at full throttle, which makes it a challenge to keep up with his energy, passion, needs, wants, and desires. He is the perfect archetype for those who just need to get things done and get them done now. There is no procrastination with this king. Even when he is blocked or reversed, slowing down is not something he knows how to do. When blocked or reversed, he just does not care where he is directing his energy, which can be both good and bad. It really depends on what needs to be achieved and what other cards you find around the reversed king.

As a spiritual influence

Fire is a very sacred element. It is used in all manner of religious and cultural ceremonies and rituals. It is used to clean, clear, and purify. There are even certain types of trees and shrubs that cannot germinate without first being burnt by fire. Just as fire can take away life, it can also give it back. The story of the phoenix is not just a wonderful legend of wishful thinking; it is a learning tool illustrating fire's life-giving potential.

In the Elder of Fire card in the Gaian Tarot, we see this sort of sacred relationship with fire at play. In burning herbs (most likely sage), to purify herself and her altar, the Elder of Fire allows us a view into a world of ritual and spiritual expansion. As the last stop along the path of wands, the king or elder knows that beyond where you now stand is nothing but rebirth. Everything you have earned, gathered, and learned is nothing more than an attachment waiting to be released. You can't take any of it with you when you return to the divine light of the ace, so here is where it all goes up in smoke, both literally and metaphorically.

Have you ever done a releasing ceremony where you have written what you want to release on paper and then burned it? I have, and so have many of my students. Throwing things into a fire can be part of a healing or part of closing a ceremony. Whatever goes into the fire is an ending to be done with, once and for all. So when this card comes up in a reading, you may need to ask yourself—what are you done with? What needs to be given to the fire? And how are you going to leave the energy of the king and be reborn into the divine spark of the Ace of Wands?

Write everything out. Write until your hands are sore, cramped, and throbbing. Take your paper and put some sage leaves in the middle. Tie it up and burn it. This very simple act of surrendering, releasing, and letting go will assist you in burning the cords of attachment that keep you bound and limited in a universe of unlimited potential.

As a messenger

Fire can be addictive. The way it burns can be both a joy to watch and a horror to behold. It all depends on what the fire is burning. When this card comes up in a reading, you may very well have to take a look at what is burning in your life. Fire grows and expands when the conditions are ripe for it to do so. If you don't have the right materials, it can be hard to sustain or build on the fire you have.

When the King of Wands appears in your reading or daily draw, you will really need to pay close attention to what is currently going on in your experience. This king's energy doesn't really dwell in the past; he moves way too fast for that. He is all about what he needs to get done now so he can move on to the next delight that awaits him. So now is where your focus will need to be. Even if you asked a question that you feel is not relevant to the present moment, the very vision of the King of Wands lets you know it actually is.

With your mind squarely focused on the now, think about where your level of attachment is. For with the King of Wands in your spread, you have more than likely become too attached to something or someone to get the result you wish to achieve. Fire needs to move; it doesn't know how to stand still. Let go of any attachments you have in making this fire grow in intensity; if you don't get it moving soon, it is guaranteed to explode.

This may mean it is also time for you to stop hiding yourself and your gifts from the world, and step into the shoes of teacher, mentor, elder, or even king. Action and forward movement are your only choices when this king makes his presence known. Resist or ignore at your own peril, for this king will leave a mark if his demands are not met.

Connecting Exercises and Spreads
What should you be leading with?

No matter our age, we all have moments in our lives when we will need to lead, be it in the work place, at home, or even just in our social circle. Sometimes the role is easy to step into and other times it is not. Stepping into this role is a twofold process.

First we need to acknowledge that the role is ours and own it. Second we need to know which leadership style is appropriate for the situation we find ourselves in. Even though most of us have a preferred way to work, teach, and take control, it is not always applicable. Being a good leader means being able to modify your style to suit the occasion or people who are relying on you.

So which king is the one that speaks to you the most? Which one do you identify with? Are you a compassionate, heart-based leader like the King of Cups? Are you a down-to-earth, hard-working, reliable leader like the King of Pentacles? Are you a strategic, long-term thinking, visionary leader like the King of Swords? Or are you just interested in getting things done and making the end result happen at any cost, like the King of Wands?

This exercise needs you to be completely honest with yourself. It doesn't matter which king you end up being, as none are better than another. When you have identified which king you are, remove your kingly alter ego from your deck and really look closely at the card. Pull out your journal or notebook and write at the very top of the page, "I am the one who ...." Now keep finishing this statement until you can't come up with another idea to finish the statement.

Here is an example of the above exercise.

The Elder of Water (Gaian Tarot)

- *I am the one who* feels at home on the water.

- *I am the one who* can safely navigate my emotions.

- *I am the one who* knows that my conditions can change quickly.

- *I am the one who* knows how to go with the flow.

- *I am the one who* understands the currents and feels the undertow.

- *I am the one who* is comfortable alone, exposed, and open to the elements.

This exercise puts you into the shoes of your card. Once you have written all you can with this card, you need to see if any of these statements show useful traits applicable to your current problem or situation. Next, place all kings face down and ask which leader you need to be right now in your life. Using that card, repeat the journal exercise with a new phrase this time. Instead of "I am the one who" you will now put at the top of your page: "I am the one who needs to be …."

Using the same card as before, here are a few example statements:

- *I am the one who needs to be* more fluid.

- *I am the one who needs to be* more in control of the direction I am headed.

- *I am the one who needs to be* aware of the conditions around me as they can change quickly.

- *I am the one who needs to be* mindful of the tides and rip currents.

Take as much time as you need with this exercise. Really dig deep and allow yourself to become one with the leader you were born to be and the elder you can become.

The Elders of the Four Directions Spread

As we have seen in the Gaian Tarot, the kings are elders of their directions and elements. Like a king, an elder is responsible for the care and well-being of its element and direction. The four directions connect us to cycles we live in externally and internally. They can represent stages of life: birth, childhood, adulthood, death; they can represent the seasons: summer, spring, autumn, winter; and of course they can be associated with the elements: air, water, fire, and earth. Pretty much any way you look at it, the four directions play a crucial part in the way we work with and relate to the tarot, especially the four kings.

In this spread, we are going to take a look and see where you are in your current life cycle. We'll examine how the elements and directions are playing out in your daily experience. As well, we'll explore how well you play elder and the four directions of your life and personal being.

For this spread, remove all four kings from your deck. Place them as illustrated in the diagram on the next page.

There are two options for the layout of the spread: one uses the Emperor as the significator, the other does not. It is up to you whether you wish to use the Emperor as a point of reflection for yourself. It will not affect the result of the cards if you do not use the Emperor in the central position.

Next, you are going to remove all the major arcana cards from your deck, as these cards show the Fool's journey from life to death. We will be using these cards to see where you are in your cycle, where you are placed on the medicine wheel, and how the four directions are assisting or challenging you right now.

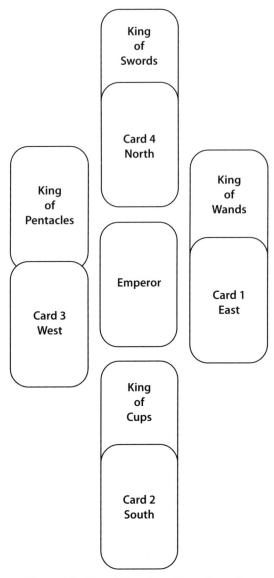

Elders of the Four Directions Spread, version 1

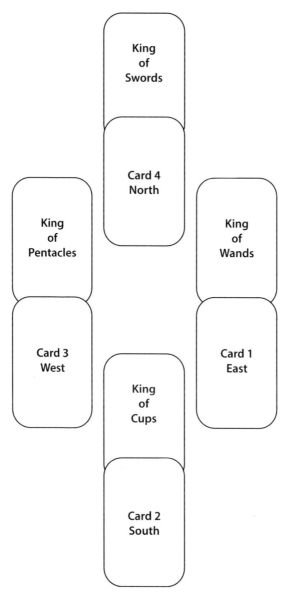

Elders of the Four Directions Spread, version 2

- *Card 1—East/beginnings*—This is where the sun rises each morning, bringing with it new energy, new possibilities, and new opportunities. The card that ends up here shows you how you deal with newness. Do you welcome new energy with open arms or does change freak you out? The card in this position illustrates how well you guard your eastern aspect and how you allow it to grow.

- *Card 2—South/action*—The south is a very social and playful direction. It is active and can show how able and willing we are to create, move, and engage with our lives. The card that ends up in this position lets you know if you are a doer or a procrastinator. This is the part of your life where you need to be flowing, not stagnating. The guardian of the south is responsible for movement, manifesting, and flow.

- *Card 3—West/letting go*—The west is often associated with fall and the energy of harvest. It is in the west that we reap what we sow and must let go of whatever no longer serves us. The card in this position lets you know how well you are able to let things go, how you deal with loss, and how much gratitude you have in your life currently. As an empowered guardian of the west, you are able to thank, bless, and release all that has come to you up until now.

- *Card 4—North/faith*—It is often said that the divine lives in the north. True north is the direction to which we are all internally pointed. Yet the north can be harsh, cold, and full of unknown experiences. Perhaps that's why it is the direction of faith. In the north, we must not allow ourselves to become attached to what we see with our eyes but have faith in the bigger vision, the inner vision, and the divine vision. This card lets you know how well you do outside of your comfort zone.

Bringing the Kingdoms Together

*Our planet is in great trouble and if we keep carrying
around old grudges and do not work together, we will all die.*

<small>CHIEF SEATTLE</small>

. . . .

Throughout this book we have looked at our court members
as individuals, not so much as members of a larger community. But like most people, the members of the tarot court
do not live in isolation; they do have to cohabitate with all the
other residents of the tarot empire. So in this chapter, you'll see
how they play, work, and interact with the rest of their tarot
citizens. We'll explore six spreads: three are sample spreads I
will walk you through, and the other three will be for you to
work through yourself.

These practice exercises will get you more comfortable with the court cards in an actual reading. None of these readings have any particular question in mind or even a designated assignment for the cards. I've done this on purpose, as I want you to start looking at the cards as telling their own stories. That said, these stories are relevant to you and your current circumstances. You will also notice I have broken these exercises up so you can read the cards in two very distinct ways: one where all the cards are about you, and one when the court card is someone else in your life.

Exercise 1: Three-Card Spread

This exercise focuses on a very simple three-card spread. This is the sort of reading you can do to start your day or set the tone for your week. Here's the sample reading:

8 of Pentacles   King of Pentacles (reversed)   4 of Cups

Exercise 1, Sample Reading 1 (Tarot of the Hidden Realm)

Reading as if the king were you

This is a really interesting set of cards, especially with the King of Pentacles in the reversed or blocked position. The 8 of Pentacles is the work card, mastering one's craft, training in one's gifts, and so on. The 4 of Cups can be considered the overwhelmed or disinterested card, which could explain why we see our king of abundance upside down. These cards could very well be letting you know that you are deliberately keeping yourself small. You are not really allowing yourself to grow, expand, and go after what you want, and it is making you feel despondent and somewhat moody.

With your king out of power, you are squandering your gifts. You are deliberately staying small, allowing fear of failure to rule your current state of abundance. In many respects, this is a selfish act that not only harms yourself but those around you as well. It's time to turn that king right side up and start seeing yourself as a leader, teacher, and mentor.

Reading as if the king were someone else

If you know for a fact that the upside-down king is not you, you will need to identify who this person is in your life. Is it a spouse, boss, work colleague, friend, or some other family member? Whoever it is, they are causing you to feel like you really have had enough. In this respect the 8 of Pentacles shows you wanting to move forward, to do more, yet you feel blocked and held back by someone who is not you, making you swim in the watery emotions of the 4 of Cups.

Just know that no one *actually* gets to block or stop you. The blockage you feel is only a matter of perspective. Your gifts are yours to do whatever you want to do with them; no one can ever take away your divine supply.

Okay, now it's your turn. Use the spread below to practice your new tarot court skills.

Page of Cups   **3 of Cups**   **4 of Pentacles**

Exercise 1, Sample Reading 2 (Tarot of the Hidden Realm)

Reading as if the page were you

_____

_____

_____

_____

_____

_____

_____

_____

_____

_____

Reading as if the page were someone else

_____

_____

_____

_____

_____

_____

_____

_____

_____

Exercise 2: Four-Card Spread

This is really very similar to the three-card spread, but for those people who like that extra card in their readings.

| Ace of Swords | 3 of Cups | Page of Wands | 6 of Swords |

Exercise 2, Sample Reading 1 (Llewellyn's Classic Tarot)

Reading as if the page were you

One of the first things I scan a reading for are pages and aces, as these cards can be seen as seeds and as beginning cards, and a page is often a key card. This spread has both, meaning it will offer both the question and the solution. In this spread I would use the Ace of Swords as the seed card, meaning here we are looking at the seed of an idea that looks to be celebrated in the 3 of Cups. It must be one fabulous idea! The Page of Wands shows us the learning curve that will be needed bringing this idea into the physical world. The 6 of Swords shows that this gift from the Ace of Swords is going to take us on a journey. As I said, this must be one incredible gift (the ace).

Remember, the Page of Wands is still learning how to use his gifts. He is pretty hit-or-miss with most of his magic. Keep this in mind as you make your way through the energy for this new journey. You might mess up, you might get a few things wrong. But if you understand that this is just the beginning and not the end, you will relax and allow yourself to settle into this new phase.

Reading as if the page were someone else

Keep in mind that pages can represent an adolescent or someone coming into sexual maturity. If you have children this age, your spread could very well be about them, which would make the 3 of Cups more of a party card. I mean this spread could literally show someone about to begin college or university. The higher learning of the ace, the partying in the 3 of Cups, the college student as the page with his potential firmly in his hands, with the journey from high school to adulthood in the 6 of Swords. Never underestimate the literal meaning of the cards.

Your turn. Here is your four-card spread:

| King of Wands | 3 of Pentacles | The Devil | 4 of Cups |

Exercise 2, Sample Reading 2 (Llewellyn's Classic Tarot)

Reading as if the king were you

_____

_____

_____

_____

_____

_____

_____

_____

_____

Reading as if the king were someone else

_____

_____

_____

_____

_____

_____

_____

_____

_____

_____

Exercise 3: Five-Card Spread

This spread is a little different than the other two. When we read this spread, we start with the center card and then work our way around the cards in a clockwise direction starting at 12 o'clock. You will also see in this sample reading there is more than one court card. Working with more than one court card at a time is a slightly advanced step, but these cards will show up in groups from time to time. So let's work our way around this spread so you can see how these cards work together.

- *Card 1*—Guardian of Water/Queen of Cups

- *Card 2*—Guardian of Fire/Queen of Wands

- *Card 3*—The Seeker/The Fool

- *Card 4*—Child of Air/Page of Swords

- *Card 5*—5 of Water/5 of Cups

Reading as if the court cards were you

In this spread we start with the central card, which just so happens to be the Queen of Cups (here, the Guardian of Water). The rest of the reading is built around the energy of this card. This queen is a deep and powerful woman. She knows how to stir things up and calm things down. In many respects, she lays the groundwork for all creative energy to be birthed into the world by giving glimpses of the past, present, and future as if they were one and the same. This queen needs good energy flow to do her magic, so let's see if the cards around her support or hinder her.

Guardian of Fire

5 of Water

Guardian of Water

The Seeker

Child of Air

Exercise 3, Sample Reading 1 (Gaian Tarot)

As her ally, we see she has the Queen of Wands (Guardian of Fire). The Queen of Wands is all about action and movement. She knows when to burst forth, heat things up, and burn through any and all obstacles. It looks like both the power of water and the energy of fire will be needed for a new start or new adventure, as seen with the Fool (here, the Seeker) card.

This journey is going to be one that will require learning, and it may require new ways of communicating needs, wants, and desires, hence the Page of Swords (Child of Air). The last card, the 5 of Cups (5 of Water) is more of a warning card that could be warning of two potential things. When you mix fire and water, you can cause harm to yourself and those around you. Also, this new journey may come at an emotional price.

This spread shows the power of a new direction or life change. It is one that is being fueled with great intensity, but it needs to be approached as if you are learning everything all over again. Old ways of thinking, being, and doing will not work for this new cycle. This need to start anew will come with a lot of mixed feelings and may require some time to grieve for what may be left behind. Just don't let this distract you from what's waiting for you.

In this reading you can see how we merged the elemental energies of the two queens together. They both offer some very powerful assistance. We then used the page as the archetype for learning and starting over. This is amplified by the presence of the Fool that came before it, as both cards let us know we find ourselves back at square one, having to start something from the beginning. The 5 of Cups is never a cheery card, but here it can actually be helpful. Leaving things behind can be sad, even if it is to make space for something better. And not paying attention to how the two queens are playing together could be disastrous. So in this respect, the 5 of Cups gives us some necessary guidance for our new journey.

Reading as if the court cards were someone else

With multiple court cards in a reading, we could very well be dealing with more than one person in a situation or circumstance. Each one of these court cards could represent a player in your life. One could very well be you, one could be someone else, and one could be the archetype you need to be in order to deal with the other person. Let's say you are the Queen of Cups but someone else is the Queen of Wands, and the Page of Swords is how the two of you need to approach one another.

Or let's say all of these court cards represent other people in your life. The Queen of Cups could be your mother, the Queen of Wands could be your sister, and the page could be your daughter. In this respect we can see that someone is going to get their feelings hurt while trying to plan a holiday or journey. Perhaps you have a family outing scheduled and your mother and sister keep butting heads about where they want to go. Your daughter is just happy to be getting out of the house, but the 5 of Cups lets you know someone is not going to be happy about compromising, meaning this could end up being a battle of power and ego.

What I've presented is only one way to read these court cards. They could also be placed in a work setting as well. Remember, this is a sample to show you how other people can and do pop up into your readings even when you don't ask about them.

Now it's your turn: take your time with the following spread. This is not a race; there is no wrong or right way to interpret the cards.

- *Card 1*—4 of Fire/4 of Wands

- *Card 2*—9 of Air/9 of Swords

- *Card 3*—Temperance

- *Card 4*—7 of Fire/7 of Wands

- *Card 5*—Guardian of Air/Queen of Swords

Reading as if the queen were you

_____

_____

_____

_____

_____

_____

_____

_____

Reading as if the queen were someone else

_____

_____

_____

_____

_____

_____

_____

_____

9 of Air

Guardian of Air

4 of Fire

Temperance

7 of Fire

Exercise 3, Sample Reading 2 (Gaian Tarot)

Exercise 4: Create Your Own Court Cards

Without a doubt, one of the best ways to truly gain a true bond to your court cards is to create your own. Now don't freak out, I don't mean you physically have to draw them! However, if you are artistically inclined, by all means—draw, paint, or Photoshop away, but you really don't need to have to draw anything. One of the best ways to create your own cards is as a collage. To do this, all you need is a stack of magazines, some glue sticks, some scissors, and some card stock. I recommend making them 5.5 x 8.5 inches, mainly because you can simply cut a standard sheet of 8.5 x 11 in half and have card stock for two cards.

Once you have your creation tools gathered, decide if you want to put yourself into the card or not. You can certainly make your own court cards with yourself as the central figure. All you need is a picture or a photocopy of a picture of yourself to place on the card. There is no wrong way or right way to do this. These cards are for you only, so if you wanna make a tarot court dedicated to yourself, go for it! If not, that's okay too.

Next, all you do is start collecting images for your cards. Perhaps you find images of water and water elements for your cups court cards; fire for your wands; food, money, houses, and jewels for your pentacles; and books, wintry scenes, mountains, and birds for your swords. Once you have your images, start gluing them to your card stock. Cut off any overhang so you can keep your cards neat and tidy.

Looking for the right sort of chalice for your cups or the perfect sword for your sword cards may take time, but that is sort of the point. As you start this exercise, you will begin as the page, making your way onto the horse of the knight, carefully creating with the queens, and then finishing your court cards as the king. This act of creating your own people cards will bring you closer to each member of the tarot royal court, as if they were all old and trusted friends. And at the end of the day, that is my wish for you: that you are able to look at each of the sixteen court cards and understand how each of them can assist or hinder you.

If you do take on this exercise and create your own cards, I would truly love to see them. I invite you to share them via Twitter or at my e-mail address, both of which are listed in the About the Author section.

This book is your introduction to the court cards but is not where your journey will end. I encourage you to explore the books in the Recommended Reading section and visit my website for upcoming classes, events, and retreats.

recommended reading

Tarot and Tarot-Related Books

Greer, Mary K. *21 Ways to Read a Tarot Card*. St. Paul, MN: Llewellyn Worldwide, 2006.

Katz, Marcus, and Tali Goodwin. *Around the Tarot in 78 Days: A Personal Journey Through the Cards*. Woodbury, MN: Llewellyn Worldwide, 2013.

Kenner, Corrine. *Tarot and Astrology: Enhance Your Readings With the Wisdom of the Zodiac*. Woodbury, MN: Llewellyn Worldwide, 2012.

Moore, Barbara. *Tarot Spreads: Layouts & Techniques to Empower Your Readings*. Woodbury, MN: Llewellyn Worldwide, 2013.

Pollack, Rachel. *The New Tarot Handbook: Master the Meaning of the Cards*. Woodbury, MN: Llewellyn Worldwide, 2013.

———. *Tarot Wisdom: Spiritual Teachings and Deeper Meanings*. Woodbury, MN: Llewellyn Worldwide, 2008.

Recommended Reading for Pages

Brown, Brene. *The Gifts of Imperfection: Let Go of Who You Think You're Supposed to Be and Embrace Who You Are*. Center City, MN: Hazelden, 2010.

Cain, Susan. *Quiet: The Power of Introverts in a World That Can't Stop Talking*. New York: Broadway Books, 2012.

Kondo, Marie. *The Life-Changing Magic of Tidying Up: The Japanese Art of Decluttering and Organizing*. Berkeley, CA: Ten Speed Press, 2014.

Recommended Reading for Knights

Gladwell, Malcolm. *Outliers: The Story of Success*. New York: Back Bay Books, 2008.

Guillebeau, Chris. *The Happiness of Pursuit: Finding the Quest That Will Bring Purpose to Your Life*. New York: Harmony Books, 2014.

Hawke, Ethan. *Rules for a Knight*. New York: Alfred A. Knopf, 2015.

Madson, Patricia Ryan. *Improve Wisdom: Don't Prepare, Just Show Up*. New York: Bell Tower, 2005.

Recommended Reading for Queens

Gilbert, Elizabeth. *Big Magic: Creative Living Beyond Fear.* New York: Riverhead Books, 2015.

Rhimes, Shonda. *Year of Yes: How to Dance It Out, Stand in the Sun and Be Your Own Person.* New York: Simon & Schuster, 2015.

Stanny, Barbara. *Sacred Success: A Course in Financial Miracles.* Dallas, TX: BenBella Books, 2014.

Recommended Reading for Kings

Calloway, Joe. *Becoming a Category of One: How Extraordinary Companies Transcend Commodity and Defy Comparison.* Hoboken, NJ: Wiley, 2003.

Cuddy, Amy. *Presence: Bringing Your Boldest Self to Your Biggest Challenges.* New York: Little, Brown and Co., 2015.

Holiday, Ryan. *The Obstacle Is the Way: The Timeless Art of Turning Trials into Triumph.* New York: Portfolio/Penguin, 2014.

Recommended Beginner Tarot Decks

Chun, Hsu Chi. *Tarot of the Magical Forest.* Torino, IT: Lo Scarabeo, 2008.

De St. Croix, Lisa. *Tarot de St. Croix.* Portland, OR: Devera Publishing, 2013.

Dugan, Ellen. *Witches Tarot*. Woodbury, MN: Llewellyn Worldwide, 2012.

Moore, Barbara, and Eugene Smith. *Llewellyn's Classic Tarot*. Woodbury, MN: Llewellyn Worldwide, 2014.

Moore, Barbara, and Aly Fell. *Steampunk Tarot*. Woodbury, MN: Llewellyn Worldwide, 2012.

Robertson, Leeza, and Eugene Smith. *Animal Totem Tarot*. Woodbury, MN: Llewellyn Worldwide, 2016.